Law Essentials

TRUSTS

D0300576

Law Essentials

TRUSTS

John Finlay, LL.B., Ph.D.
Senior Lecturer in Law,
University of Glasgow

DUNDEE UNIVERSITY PRESS
2012

Published in Great Britain in 2012 by
Dundee University Press
University of Dundee
Dundee DD1 4HN

www.dundee.ac.uk/dup

ISBN 978–1–84586–129–2

No natural forests were destroyed to make this product;
only farmed timber was used and replanted

British Library Cataloguing-in-Publication data
A catalogue for this book is available on request from the British Library.

Typeset by Koinonia, Bury
Printed by Bell & Bain Ltd, Glasgow

CONTENTS

TABLE OF CASES

TABLE OF STATUTES

1 INTRODUCTION

WHAT IS A TRUST?

In Scots law the legal concept of the trust has a long history of development and, over that time, has come to take on a number of characteristics. However, there is no single definition of a trust that covers every example of the trust relationship. For the purpose of this book we may define a trust as a situation where one party, a "trustee", owns certain property which he must hold and administer on behalf of another party, a "beneficiary", in order to accomplish certain purposes. The purposes will usually be defined by a party called the "truster".

The essence of a trust is the relationship between the trustee and the beneficiary. This involves a fiduciary obligation. The trustee must discharge his duty to administer the property in good faith, regardless of his own personal interests, for the benefit (or "behoof", to use an old word) of the beneficiary. This duty qualifies the ownership which the trustee has of the trust property (although his title is an absolute one). It may be thought of as a burden on his title, preventing him from dealing with the trust property as though it were his own private property.

A trust in itself is neither a legal person nor a corporation. The modern analysis of the Scottish trust stresses the idea that the trustee holds two "patrimonies" or estates: his private patrimony (his own rights and liabilities) and the trust patrimony (the rights and liabilities of the trust estate). These are seen as separate legal entities. Therefore if the trustee's private patrimony becomes vulnerable to his personal creditors, because he cannot meet his debts, the separate entity that is the trust patrimony is protected.

WHY USE A TRUST?

There are many reasons why a person may try to protect assets by placing them in trust. In a trust, the person or persons with the ultimate right to benefit from the trust are not the same persons who own the trust property for the time being or who are charged with its management. Trust property is protected from the personal creditors of the truster and the trustees. It is possible to impose conditions on the right to benefit from the trust, setting up some contingency that must be met before the property will be handed over, or to delay the handing over of property for a period of time during which it is administered by trustees. All of these attributes may be useful to a potential truster.

Personal or family reasons

One reason for creating a trust may be ease of administration. If the truster is in ill health, or intends to travel the world or to retire abroad, then he may place his assets in trust to avoid the burden of having to manage them or to do so at a distance.

A second reason may be to establish a fund for the protection of a vulnerable person. A child, or an adult who lacks legal capacity, is not capable of dealing with property and their economic needs can be met by setting up a trust for their benefit. This would particularly be the case where a trust is set up on the death of a parent, where the property will be managed by trustees in the interests of the child or incapable adult. Similarly, an adult, though legally competent, may be protected from himself by means of a trust. This was common in the 18th century and can still be done today where someone lacks the financial skills to deal with their property sensibly. A trust may be set up in which trustees administer the property and ensure that the improvident beneficiary is properly maintained.

A family of means may use a trust in order to protect its wealth down the generations. A private family trust will allow each generation to benefit from the income generated by family assets, but will ensure that those assets are not dissipated by one generation at the expense of the succeeding ones. Traditionally, there may be reasons of tax efficiency in doing this, since it may have avoided inheritance tax. A trust, like a corporation, need never die.

A third reason may be that there is some uncertainty and a trust can be used pending the resolution of that uncertainty. For instance, the truster may wish an asset to go to X "if and when" X reaches a certain age. If the condition is not satisfied, then the truster may wish the asset to go elsewhere. Similarly, if a class of beneficiaries is named (for example "my surviving children") with payment of the asset delayed to a particular date or event, the population of the class would be determined at that future time and may be not be the same as it was on the day the trust came into effect.

A typical arrangement (which, up to 2006, enjoyed tax benefits) for the use of a trust to aid children on an ongoing basis has been the accumulation and maintenance trust. The truster would hand over a fund to trustees who would maintain and invest it and ensure that regular payments were made to the truster's children to meet their living and educational needs until a specified time (usually the end of the child's participation in fulltime education).

Improper liferents

A particular use of the trust is in the context of an improper liferent (sometimes called a beneficiary liferent). In contrast, a proper liferent does not involve a trust at all. A proper liferent involves the disposition or gift of property (called the fee) to a liferenter and a fiar. The liferenter has a real right in the property which gives him the right to possess it and enjoy its fruits. This is not ownership, however, and it is subject to certain obligations: for example that the liferenter pay any ordinary burdens or taxes associated with the fee and pay for its normal upkeep. The liferenter cannot destroy the property itself and must preserve its substance, drawing from it only the income or fruits. The fiar has the real right of the ownership in the property but, for the duration of the liferent, his ownership is subject to the liferenter's lesser real right.

In an improper liferent, the fee is conveyed to trustees who administer it in accordance with a trust purpose that would involve the payment of the income from the fee to the liferenter and the fee itself to the fiar. In these circumstances, the liferenter has only a personal right against the trustees for payment of the income in accordance with the trust purpose. The trustees are bound eventually to convey the fee to the fiar but they must do so in accordance with the trust purpose.

An improper liferent is very flexible. At the commencement of the liferent, the identity of the fiars may not yet have been ascertained. The truster may even give his trustees the discretion to determine who will eventually become the fiars. To understand the concept of liferent and fee it is necessary to bear in mind two things. First, the fee can be any type of property except property that is consumed in use. So, the fee might be a house (in which case there may be rental income) or it might be a fleet of cars (again, with income from hiring them out) or a portfolio of shares (generating dividend income). Second, the truster can determine when the fee vests (see "Vesting" below).

Vesting

A right is vested when it becomes an asset in someone's estate. If a right has vested in X's estate, that means that if X dies, his heir is entitled to that right. If the right had not yet vested, X's heir would have no claim to it. To have a vested right, therefore, is to have an indefeasible right: a right that cannot be defeated even by one's own death. Such a right may be diluted but not removed.

Vesting is an important concept in the law of trusts and in succession. Vesting may occur *a morte testatoris* (by the death of the testator) or the testator may direct that vesting should take place at a later date or on the happening of a specific event. Vesting cannot pre-date the payment of the fee but vesting and payment can take place simultaneously. For example, a truster may wish to create on his death a liferent interest in favour of his spouse while leaving the fee to his children. The fee might vest on the truster's death, with payment of the fee to be made on the death of the liferentrix, or the fee may vest only at the expiry of the liferent with the direction that it be paid to such of the truster's children who survive to that date. If so, and one of the children does not survive, then that child's heirs would have no vested right to inherit, since the contingency of survival had not been met. Trustees would have the power to make payment only to those who enjoyed a vested right

Vesting may be subject to defeasance. This will occur if vesting has taken place but the right that is vested is subsequently diluted by the addition of further owners of the fee. For example, suppose that the testator leaves the fee to his children equally and a liferent to his wife. The fee is to vest immediately on the testator's death, with payment postponed until the end of the liferent. At that point, the testator has two children, therefore each child has a vested right to half of the fee. Suppose, however, that a posthumous child is born a few months later. The half-share of the elder children will be partially defeated since the third child will also have a vested right to an equal share of the fee. Each child now has a one-third share of the fee which will be paid at the expiry of the liferent.

Alimentary liferents

Special rules apply to an alimentary liferent. This is a liferent set up in order to provide the liferenter with subsistence during childhood or his education. An alimentary liferent is protected from the liferenter's creditors, at least in so far as it is not excessive in regard to the amount paid for his maintenance. The second peculiarity is that, once the liferenter accepts an alimentary liferent, it cannot be renounced. However, the provision which created the liferent may be varied or revoked (see Chapter 8). The liferent may cease to be alimentary in nature: for instance, once full-time education is complete, the liferent will continue as an ordinary liferent and the special rules will cease to apply.

Public and charitable reasons

A trust may be set up for charitable reasons in order to benefit the public. In the 18th century it was not uncommon for people to set up a trust the purpose of which was to fund a bursary for young scholars studying subjects such as philosophy or divinity at university. A particular asset might also be placed in trust. Perhaps some park land might be placed in trust in order to preserve it as a recreational space for the public. After a disaster of some kind, it may be convenient to set up a trust in order to administer funds received as donations from the public.

Charitable trusts have traditionally been common and they have not disappeared with the advent of the registered charity. Such trusts must benefit the public, or a section of the public, and there are some rules about how their purposes may be defined.

Commercial uses of trusts

Trusts have many potential uses in the commercial world. Primarily this is because assets held in trust fall into the trust patrimony of the trustees. This means that they are not vulnerable to the personal creditors of the trustees whose private estates, the personal patrimonies which they each own, are quite separate from the property they own as trustees. Assets held in trust are generally safe provided that the trustees act properly and do not abuse their fiduciary position.

Commercially, trusts have often been used in debt factoring and in securitisation arrangements. A trust can be used in debt factoring in order to overcome the difficulty that the legal transfer of a large number of debts held by a single creditor would require the individual assignation of each debt followed by intimation to each debtor. Thus, suppose that Mortgages-R-Us Ltd holds £50 million worth of debt which, as creditor, it is due to be paid by its many debtors over the next 10 years. Rather than wait to collect that money, which it would then lend out to new debtors, it sells those debts at a discount to Credit Collectors Ltd. A convenient method of transferring these book debts is for Mortgages-R-Us simply to declare that it is holding the debts in trust for Credit Collectors Ltd, thus transferring its right to the debts and to all rights arising under the debts. The latter thus would have paid for the right to become beneficiaries to this income and, usually, the customers of Mortgages-R-Us would be none the wiser. This is good from the truster/trustee company's perspective, for another reason: it does not risk its customers gaining the impression that a sale, which was in the normal course of business, was actually carried out for another reason, such as that the company had cash-flow problems.

Trusts can often be found used in the construction industry. A funder (public or private) may wish to pay a building company to develop a new road or housing estate and, to counter the commercial risk of the liquidation of the building company, it would make sense to place the funding in trust. From the building company's perspective, this would guarantee payment for the project in the event that the funder himself fell into financial difficulties. The trustee (typically, a bank) would then periodically remit payments as and when stages of the development were completed to the funder's satisfaction.

A trust might be used to protect a company from a hostile takeover. Shares may be placed in trust by their owner in order to ensure that no-one can obtain a controlling shareholding in the company. There may be a commercial reason this or, for example in the case of a professional football club, the desire to protect the club as a business from the machinations of a single wealthy owner. The Scottish Law Commission (*Discussion Paper on Accumulation of Income and Lifetime of Private Trusts* (Scot Law Com No 142, 2010), para 5.5) has asked whether the phrase "commercial trust" should be given a specific definition in Scots law.

A recent development is the private purposes trust, generally a commercial vehicle which need not have any beneficiaries at all. The trust exists to achieve defined purposes and, in effect, would be the private equivalent of non-charitable public trusts. The Scottish Law Commission has also consulted on whether to introduce these in Scotland (*Discussion Paper on Supplementary and Miscellaneous Issues relating to Trust Law* (Scot Law Com No 148, 2011), Chapter 12).

Statutory trusts

Sometimes trusts are created in statute for particular purposes. The best-known example of this is in the Bankruptcy (Scotland) Act 1985. When a person is insolvent, a petition may be brought for the appointment by a sheriff of an interim or permanent trustee in sequestration under s 2 of the Act. The role of the trustee, defined in s 3, includes ascertaining the assets and liabilities of the debtor, recovering the debtor's estate and distributing it among the creditors according to their respective entitlements. They work under the supervision of an officer of the court known as the Accountant in Bankruptcy (whose function is defined in s 1A of the 1985 Act).

Another example arises in the context of a standard security. The creditor, once he has carried out the various procedural steps that allow the sale of the security subjects, holds the proceeds in trust for the debtor under s 27(1) of the Conveyancing and Feudal Reform (Scotland) Act 1970. He is bound to pay over any residue to the debtor after payment of expenses and any secured creditors. The statutory trust relates only to the proceeds once the subjects have been sold. Since the right in security held by a creditor is a *jus in re aliena* (a right held in someone else's property), the creditor cannot be a trustee of the subjects themselves since it is impossible to own an asset and, at the same time, have a right in security in it (see G L Gretton, "Constructive Trusts" (1997) Edin LR 281 at 289).

THE CLASSIFICATION OF TRUSTS

Not only do trusts have many uses, but there are many ways to classify them. These may depend on the mode of creation of the trust, or the purpose of the trust or the nature of the beneficiaries. However they are classified, a particular trust may easily cross over into more than one category.

Standard trust

The phrase "standard trust" has no legal meaning, but it has been used by the Scottish Law Commissioners to provide a paradigmatic example of the Scottish trust. It refers to an express *inter vivos* trust (on which, see p 10) involving a tripartite relationship between a truster, a trustee and a beneficiary. It is worth setting out what these roles involve. The truster creates the trust and defines what its purposes should be. This may involve creating a written deed of trust. The trustee, or trustees, who agree to act must follow those purposes when administering the trust property. That property belongs to them jointly as trustees, although it does not become their personal property as individuals. The beneficiary has a personal right to receive the trust property in conformity with the truster's intention as set out in the trust purposes. Unlike under the law of contract, a personal right may be acquired by a beneficiary without his consent or even without his knowledge (the beneficiary may even be yet unborn).

In any trust, ownership of trust assets vests in the trustees. This means that the property must pass to them from the truster. If it does not, it remains vulnerable to the truster's creditors. In regard to moveable property, title will pass by means of delivery. Where the property is heritable (ie land or buildings) title passes only when a disposition is registered in the Land Register. Where the property is incorporeal, then the process of transfer is by assignation and intimation. Assignation alone is not sufficient to pass title, nor is the mere delivery of a disposition. Registration and intimation are regarded as equivalents, for land and incorporeal property, to delivery which is essential to transfer title to moveable property at common law.

A truster-as-trustee trust

This phrase is also used by the Scottish Law Commission but it is again a purely descriptive one. It refers to a situation where the truster and the sole trustee are the same person. What is special about it is the mode of creation, since it involves an owner of property declaring that he no longer owns it as an individual, dealing with it in his own interest, but as a trustee who owns the property, and administers it, on behalf of a beneficiary. This kind of trust raises issues of proof, since it would be easy for someone to claim to his creditors that some of the assets he held were not his own property but were actually trust property. No actual conveyance of property is involved, but some equivalent is necessary in order for the truster to move the asset from his private patrimony to the trust patrimony. A private patrimony is the sum of an individual's personal legal rights and liabilities. A trust patrimony consists of the assets of the trust together with any liabilities incurred by the trustees in the administration of the trust. These patrimonies are separate legal entities. While the "dual patrimony" theory has been developed not by the courts but by Scottish Law Commissioners, it is one that is consistent with the general principles of Scots law.

The truster who becomes sole trustee must create a trust by doing something that indicates that the assets placed in trust have moved from his private patrimony to the trust patrimony. Intimation to a beneficiary that the trust has been created is regarded as sufficient.

Express trusts

A truster may create a trust expressly, orally or in writing. Most trusts, in fact, are expressly created, with the purposes set down in a written deed of trust. Some kinds of trust, particularly where the property involved is heritable property, can only be created when written in a legally valid document. A *mortis causa* trust must always be in writing since it is created in a testamentary writing. Whether oral or written, however, some express act of creation – a declaration of trust – is necessary to create the trust, although, until title to the trust property has actually been transferred to the trustees, the property remains vulnerable to the creditors of the truster. An alternative view of the creation of the trust exists, which suggests that the trust is not created until title to its property has been conveyed to the trustees. This issue is discussed further in Chapter 2.

Implied trusts

Apart from express creation, it is said that a trust may be created by implication in certain circumstances. This is controversial, since it is not clear in exactly what circumstances an implied trust may arise. It has been suggested that the following two types of implied trust exist.

Trusts created by inference

The first type of so-called implied trust is really an express trust in which the declaration of trust, rather than being clearly expressed, must be inferred from the words used by the truster. This is simply a question of interpretation. The court, if satisfied that the language used, in the context, was sufficiently clear that it imposed an obligation on someone to carry out a task in favour of a third party, may regard it as demonstrating the intention to create a trust. There is no implication in this case. The trust arises based on the expressed intention of the truster, however lacking in clarity the expression of that intention.

An example of this kind of trust is the so-called "precatory trust". This is a voluntarily created trust where the trust must be inferred from the words used in circumstances where the ordinary meaning of those words suggests a request rather than a command. In fact, what is being inferred is an intention by the truster to create an express trust. Therefore the judges in *Reid's Trs v Dawson* (1915) came to the view that when the truster, in the context of that case, said that he would "prefer" something to happen, he meant to impose an obligation so that it did happen. The language he used was read as a direction. In other words, it was an express trust purpose. If the language is truly "precatory" (meaning that it communicates a mere wish or desire, rather than a command or direction), then it cannot form a trust purpose since it cannot be inferred from the language that there was ever any intention to impose an obligation. Therefore a "precatory trust" is a contradiction in terms: if a "precatory trust" is a trust, it is not because the words used are precatory but because they are not. The courts tend to the view that precatory words addressed to an executor will usually be regarded as imposing a binding obligation, whereas when addressed to a legatee they will not (W A Wilson and A G M Duncan, *Trusts, Trustees and Executors* (1995), para 2.13).

Involuntary trusts

The second type of implied trust is said to arise from trusts that are involuntary. They are created automatically by operation of law in certain fact situations and therefore they are created independently of the will of the truster.

An example of this which is sometimes given is the resulting trust. This is a trust in which the purposes fail but assets remain that have not been distributed. The presumption may then arise (unless the truster has excluded it) that the trustee, rather than holding the trust property for the beneficiaries, holds it purely for the purpose of returning it to the truster or his representatives. However, it has been seriously doubted whether resulting trusts are involuntary or, indeed, whether they are a separate type of trust at all. They might be viewed as being the consequence of an implied term, to be read into every private trust, that "a contingent beneficial right is established in favour of the truster, the contingency being purified in the event of the failure of the trust purposes at a time when there are still trusts assets" (Gretton (1997) (above), pp 309–310). A resulting trust, on this argument, is not a type of trust at all. It is simply a presumption that the truster intends the trustee, should the trust purposes fail, to hold the property for his benefit. The presumption might be rebutted. This would be the case where the truster made it sufficiently clear that it was his intention to divest himself of the title to the trust property permanently.

Another example of an involuntary trust is the constructive trust which is discussed in Chapter 2. This is said to arise when a certain relationship comes into being between parties; however, the law in regard to constructive trusts is very unclear.

Inter vivos and mortis causa trusts

An *inter vivos* trust is one established among the living, with the intention that it take effect during the lifetime of the truster. A *mortis causa* trust, sometimes called a testamentary trust, is one created in contemplation of the death of the truster, with the intention that it take effect on or after his death.

Private and public trusts

A private trust is one intended to benefit a specified person or group of individuals. A typical private trust is a family trust for the benefit of the truster's descendents, or a trust for the friends of the truster. The key element is the intention to benefit a restricted group.

In contrast, a public trust is one intended to benefit the public in general or a section of the public. Rather than being set up to benefit those with a connection to the truster, public trusts are set up to carry forward an intention to provide a benefit more generally. For example, while particular individuals suffering financial distress will benefit under a public trust, the truster's objective was not to benefit those individuals but rather to promote the relief of poverty among the public or a section of the public. It is in this sense that the trust is public. One consequence of this is that there is a greater role for the courts in regard to the administration of public trusts, where the public interest may require to be protected, than there is in private trusts. Therefore any variation of the purposes of a public trust will generally require judicial intervention.

However, it can sometimes be difficult to distinguish between a public trust and a private trust. A classic illustration of this is *Salvesen's Trs v Wye* (1954) in which a testator left a legacy to his "poor relatives, friends or acquaintances". This might have been a public trust, since the class to be benefited was a wide one. However, the court held that the dominant factor was the connection which the class of beneficiaries had with the testator, rather than the fact that they were poor, therefore this was a private trust.

A clear distinction between public and private trusts relates to the question of who has the right to bring an action against the trustees. In a private trust, the truster (if still alive) and all the beneficiaries have title to sue to ensure that the trust purposes are carried out. In a public trust, any identifiable or potential beneficiary may sue. The Lord Advocate has a general public interest role in litigation and may intervene to bring an action with regard to a public trust. The Lord Advocate still has a potential role in public (non-charitable) trusts under the Law Reform (Miscellaneous Provisions) (Scotland) Act 1990. However, supervisory powers which the Lord Advocate formerly exercised under that Act in respect of public trusts which were, or held themselves out to be, charities have been replaced by those of the Office of the Scottish Charity Regulator. There is also some suggestion, although no clear authority, that a public trust may be enforced by an *actio popularis* (A Mackenzie Stuart, *The Law of Trusts* (1932), p 110). In other words, any member of the public may have the right to sue to enforce the trust purposes of a public trust.

A further distinction between a public trust and a private one is the attitude of the courts. Public trusts are entitled to receive a benign construction. This means that the court will be more forgiving when it comes to interpreting trust purposes in a public trust than in a private one and, in effect, will do what it properly can to save a trust set up for public purposes from invalidity. The extent of this is uncertain. Small, technical difficulties will be more readily overlooked in regard to the purposes of a public trust than a private one. The use of vague words, for instance, may be seen as sufficient in some cases because of the general intention of the truster to benefit the public. Thus a trust set up "for charitable purposes" is not invalid due to uncertainty despite the potential width of meaning of that phrase.

Discretionary trusts

This is not really a separate category of trust in Scots law. However, the discretion of trustees can be very important in the administration of a trust, regardless of whether the trust is a private or a public one. The truster, for example, may define a class of persons who are to benefit but, within that class, grant to the trustees the power to select which members actually benefit. How much each beneficiary receives, and when their share of the trust property vests in them, are also matters that may be left to the discretion of trustees. The trustees, in other words, use their discretion to determine the extent of the rights of individual beneficiaries.

As well as having discretion in regard to how to dispose of the trust estate (referred to as "dispositive discretion"), trustees may have discretion in regard to the administration of the estate (sometimes called "administrative discretion"). This relates to the everyday running of the trust, including such matters as when and where to hold a meeting, whether to sell trust property or whether to make a particular investment decision.

Any trustee enjoys administrative discretion, but some types of trustee may lack dispositive discretion. For example, there may be a question mark against the use of such discretion by a judicial factor, appointed by the court to administer a trust estate in the absence of any trustees. Since the court cannot exercise discretion on behalf of trustees (see Chapter 5) then a judicial factor, who is appointed by and represents the court, may not. This would certainly be the case where it is clear that the truster nominated trustees specifically for their personal characteristics (*delectus personae*), since this suggests that the exercise of discretion was intended to be personal to those trustees.

Trusts for administration

A trust for administration is a trust set up with no purposes other than that the trustee holds property for the benefit of a beneficiary or, if more than one, for several beneficiaries in common. The beneficiaries in such a trust can insist at any point on the property being conveyed to them. Once the trust is created, the beneficiaries cannot be changed and they have an absolute and immediate right to the property and income of the trust. Such a trust is often called a "bare" trust or a "simple" trust.

Essential Facts

- A trust is a tripartite relationship involving one or more trusters, trustees and beneficiaries.
- The trust is very flexible and has many uses, commercial and non-commercial.
- Trusts may be public or private and, while usually created expressly, may arise involuntarily in certain circumstances.
- Trusts may be created on the death of the truster or during his lifetime and the truster may give very wide discretion to the trustees in terms of both administration and distribution of the trust estate.

2 THE CREATION OF A TRUST

Usually, a trust will be created by a truster on a voluntary basis. The traditional view is that this requires two stages. First, there must be a declaration of trust by the truster in favour of a trustee or trustees and, second, this must be followed by the transfer of ownership in the trust property from the truster to the trustee(s). This results in the trustees becoming fiduciaries, owning the property for the benefit not of themselves but of beneficiaries, or a class of beneficiaries, nominated by the truster. Trust is therefore a tripartite relationship. For it to exist there must be at least one truster, at least one trustee and at least one beneficiary. The traditional view has been questioned and it has been suggested that the declaration of trust (a written or, in some cases, oral statement indicating that a trust is being set up) is all that is required to create a trust in Scots law. More will be said on this below.

THE TRUSTER

The creation of a trust requires a truster with legal capacity. Anyone lacking this, such as a person under the age of 12 or someone of unsound mind, cannot be a truster. A person aged 12 or older can apparently create a *mortis causa* trust, but not an *inter vivos* trust: Age of Legal Capacity (Scotland) Act 1991, s 2(2). A person aged 16 or 17 has capacity to create an *inter vivos* trust but may apply to the court to have this set aside, provided that this is done before he attains the age of 21 and he can establish that it was a prejudicial transaction, ie one which an adult, exercising reasonable prudence, would not have entered in the same circumstances (1991 Act, s 3).

A truster may be a natural or a juristic person. A corporation or a partnership can be a truster. A truster can be the sole trustee or the sole beneficiary. A truster can also be one of the trustees and the sole beneficiary. The only legally impossible combination is where the same person purports to be the sole trustee and the sole beneficiary since, under the doctrine of confusion, any such trust would be extinguished.

INTER VIVOS AND *MORTIS CAUSA* TRUSTS

The declaration of trust may be *inter vivos* (literally, among the living) or *mortis causa* (in contemplation of death). The former, as mentioned in the previous chapter, involves a trust that will take effect during the lifetime of the truster; the latter, also known as a testamentary trust, is intended to take effect on or after the truster's death. A *mortis causa* trust cannot, therefore, be revoked by the truster, since it does not exist until he is dead. The testamentary writing containing the direction to create the trust, however, can be revoked at any time prior to death unless the testator has entered into an obligation not to do so.

REQUIREMENTS OF WRITING (SCOTLAND) ACT 1995

While it would be unwise for anyone to set up a trust other than in written form, the relevant legislation, the Requirements of Writing (Scotland) Act 1995, *requires* a trust to be in writing only in the following circumstances:

(a) where the truster declares that he is sole trustee of his own property or any property which he may acquire (s 1(2)(a)(iii));
(b) where the trust relates to "an interest in land" (s 1(2)(b)); or
(c) where the trust is created by a testamentary disposition (s 1(2)(c)).

An "interest in land" is not defined but it will include any rights *in rem* such as ownership, heritable securities, servitudes, leases for more than one year, and liferents. A *mortis causa* trust will be in formal writing; an *inter vivos* trust need not be, unless (a) or (b) above pertains.

Where the truster is sole trustee, he must intimate the written declaration of trust to the beneficiary. This puts the matter out of the truster's hands, although, so far as the rest of the world is concerned, the trust may be latent (or hidden and unknown). Where a truster who is sole trustee does not use writing, but makes an oral declaration in favour of a beneficiary, it is possible that a trust may still be created under subss 1(3) and (4) of the 1995 Act. By these provisions, if the beneficiary has acted or refrained from acting in reliance on the trust, with the knowledge and acquiescence of the truster, then the truster will not be able to withdraw from the trust, provided that: (a) the beneficiary's position has already been affected to a material extent; and (b) it would be adversely affected to a material extent if the truster withdrew.

VOLUNTARY TRUSTS

The declaration of trust

The declaration of trust requires no particular form of words but should specify the purposes of the trust; nominate the trustee(s) and the beneficiary or beneficiaries; and identify the trust property. A bequest of a share of property "to A for behoof of B" will be construed, unless there is any indication to the contrary, as the constitution of a trust in favour of B.

On one view, as soon as the declaration of trust is made, the trust is created (see "When is a trust born?"). The more traditional view is that the trust is not created until ownership in the trust property is transferred to the trustee. However, conceptually, the traditional view does not explain what should be done with property which the truster does not yet own but intends to acquire. He cannot transfer ownership, since he currently lacks ownership, but it would be consistent with the law of succession, for example, to imagine a testator leaving property in trust which he does not yet own since it is possible to leave a legacy of property which one did not own at death and, indeed, never owned.

Precatory words

The words used in the declaration must be clear and sufficient in their terms to indicate that a trust has been created. In the case of *mortis causa* trusts especially, the meaning of a term which purports to leave property to a beneficiary might not always be clear. Sometimes, the language might be regarded merely as precatory, ie expressing a general wish that something should happen, as opposed to laying down a specific instruction that it be so. In such a case, the testator may not have succeeded in creating a trust (see, further, Chapter 1).

Transfer of ownership

On the traditional view, it is necessary for the creation of a trust that ownership (a real right) of the trust property should pass from the truster to the trustee or trustees. How this is done depends on the nature of the property being transferred. If it is heritable property, a valid disposition in favour of the trustees must be registered in the Land Register of Scotland. Mere delivery of the disposition to the trustees does not pass ownership in the same way that the assignation of an incorporeal right does not pass title without the necessary step of intimation to the debtor. The ownership of moveable property is transferred at common law by physical delivery.

In the case of a sole truster who becomes sole trustee, physical delivery is impossible. The courts have accepted in this situation that intimation of the trust to the beneficiary is the equivalent of delivery of trust property to the trustee. Clearly, the intimation must identify what the trust property is. As we have seen, in this situation there must be a written declaration of trust.

The underlying idea behind the requirement that property be transferred is that the truster is being divested of title in that property and the title is being invested in the trustee or trustees. In effect, the truster is putting the property out of his personal patrimony, and so beyond the reach of his creditors, and into the trust patrimony in which the beneficiaries have a personal right.

The "dual patrimony" theory

At the point that the truster is divested of ownership of the property that is being placed in trust, it ceases to be vulnerable to his personal creditors. Trust property is not vulnerable to the personal creditors of the trustees: *Heritable Reversionary Co Ltd v Millar* (1892). However, it is vulnerable to the creditors of the trust. To appreciate this distinction, it is necessary to understand that a trustee has two patrimonies: his personal estate and the trust estate. He deals with trust property not in his own right but purely in his capacity as a trustee (or, as some lawyers say, *qua* trustee). A truster who becomes sole trustee, therefore, continues to own the trust assets but shifts them from his personal patrimony to the trust patrimony: he ceases to own them as an individual and owns them as a trustee for the benefit of a beneficiary.

If debts are incurred on the trust estate while the trustee administers it as part of his trust patrimony, then the creditors have recourse against that estate and not against the trustee personally. When the trust estate is exhausted, the trustees have no personal liability for debts incurred in the proper course of its administration. In other words, trust property owned by the trustee in his trust patrimony is, usually, vulnerable to trust creditors to its full extent. This does not extend to assets in the trustee's personal patrimony. These are his personal property and quite separate. The assets in this general or private patrimony are therefore only vulnerable to the personal creditors of the trustee. This idea is known as the "dual patrimony" theory (K G C Reid, "Patrimony not equity" (2000) 3 *European Review of Private Law* 427). It is a theory because, as yet, while it makes sense of the established principles of Scots law, there is no judicial approval of it (*The Nature and Constitution of Trusts* (Scot Law Com Discussion Paper No 133, 2006), para 2.26). However, it has the support of the Scottish Law Commission.

The concept is straightforward. If there is one trustee, he owns both his personal patrimony and the trust patrimony. If there is more than one trustee, each owns his personal patrimony and they jointly own the trust patrimony. Although two patrimonies may be owned by one person, the patrimonies themselves are distinct legal entities and should be kept separate: assets from one should not be transferred to the other. Receipts from sales of trust property, for example, should go into the trust patrimony only and debts incurred in the proper administration of the trust are debts of the trust patrimony only. What each trustee might do as a private individual affects their personal patrimony and not the trust property which, as a group, the body of trustees together own jointly.

Ownership of the trust fund

Trustees own trust property as fiduciaries, ie they own it outright, but only for the benefit (or, to use an old Scots word, the "behoof") of the beneficiaries. Trust property is owned jointly by the trustees and the beneficiaries have no more than a personal right to the property. This personal right is important, since it allows the beneficiary to compel the trustee to carry out the trust purposes and to bring an action for breach of trust or one for count, reckoning and payment. However, the beneficiary has no real right in the trust property unless and until it is actually conveyed to him by the trustees. Joint property is not the same as common property, but since the fact that trust property is held jointly is relevant to how that property is administered, the consequences of this are discussed in Chapter 5.

When is a trust born?

Since the Scottish Law Commission (Scot Law Com No 133, para 2.2) has distinguished three types of trust, it is useful to do so here. They are:

(1) the "standard" trust. This is an *inter vivos* trust set up by the truster to take effect in his lifetime, in which one or more trustees own and administer the property for the benefit of one or more beneficiaries;

(2) the *mortis causa* trust;

(3) the "truster-as-trustee" trust, in which the truster is sole trustee for the benefit of one or more beneficiaries.

The "standard" trust

In theory, this trust is created as soon as two consecutive events have taken place. First, the truster has made a declaration of trust. Second, the truster has transferred the trust property to the trustees. Once this has happened, the beneficiaries acquire a vested personal right to the trust property and the trustees are under a duty to act in accordance with the trust purposes.

If the would-be trustees neglect to complete title to the property assigned
or disponed to them – in other words, if they fail to intimate an assignation
of incorporeal property or to register a disposition of heritable property
in the Land Register – then the beneficiary can have no vested personal
right. This is simply because there is no trust: the property, after all, has
not successfully passed to the trustees.

The mortis causa trust

This trust is constituted at the death of the truster. The usual rule is that the
beneficiary under a testamentary deed acquires a vested right as soon as the
testator dies (unless vesting is postponed). In contrast to the standard trust,
no transfer of title to the testator's executor is necessary for this to happen;
the law does not wait for the trustee to complete title to the trust estate.
Although the trust cannot exist prior to the truster's death, the truster may
incur liability if he had promised the beneficiary that he would set up a
mortis causa trust. This will usually be a unilateral obligation, and therefore
the promise must be contained in a written document subscribed by the
truster: Requirements of Writing (Scotland) Act 1995, s 2(a)(ii). If it is,
the beneficiary in whose favour it was made may sue the truster's estate for
breach of promise.

The "truster-as-trustee" trust

This trust is not created merely by the declaration of trust. The truster must
communicate the declaration to a beneficiary. If this were not the case, then
there is nothing to stop a person defeating the claims of his personal creditors by producing a written declaration of trust and claiming that an asset
he owns is actually held in trust for another (known as a "latent" trust).
Communication to a beneficiary, however, provides limited protection to
the creditor in this situation. Nonetheless, it is a step the truster must take
and this should put matters beyond his sole control since the beneficiary
will gain a vested personal right.

The alternative theory to that of the standard trust

The theory of the creation of the trust has not been fully developed by
the Scottish courts. The Scottish Law Commission, not satisfied with the
traditional view of the creation of the standard trust, has proposed an alternative. This is that a standard trust is created not when the trust property
is delivered to the trustee(s), but when the declaration of trust is communicated to the trustee. This is the "point of no return" for the truster and
the point from which the trustee can demand that the trust property be
transferred into the trustee's trust patrimony. The trust will be created only

when, and if, at least one trustee accepts office. The declinature of office by prospective trustees is a sign that a trust may not be one that could be viably or reasonably administered, and it is thought undesirable that a trust should come into existence unless a trustee accepts office. If no trustee accepts office, in other words, the truster may try to constitute the trust again and no beneficiary would be able to enforce the original declaration.

This analysis brings trusts of type (2) and (3) above into conformity with those of type (1). Death, in a *mortis causa* trust, is the ultimate "point of no return". Intimation of a declaration to a beneficiary (in the truster-as-trustee trust) and intimation of the declaration of trust to the trustee (in the alternative theory) also represent "points of no return" so far as the truster is concerned. None of these events relies on the transfer of ownership of property to create the trust. This therefore removes from the birth of a trust a process which, to the risk of the beneficiary, might be negligently or even deliberately postponed by the trustee's failure to make intimation or registration.

The consequence of this analysis is that, once the declaration of trust is made and communicated to the trustee, the trust property remains vulnerable to the creditors of the truster. However, the trustees will be in a position to compel transfer of that property to themselves and, in the event of the bankruptcy of the truster, the trustees will rank as personal creditors. This offers a measure of protection to the beneficiaries which the traditional analysis does not.

Acquirenda

A truster can put into trust items of property he does not yet own but has a personal right to acquire. Since the right to receive future property is incorporeal in nature, its transfer must be effected by assignation and intimation. To complete the transfer of the right, the trustees (the assignees) must intimate the assignation of the right by the truster (the cedent) to the debtor (ie the party bound to transfer the asset to the truster).

The latent trust

The creation of a trust in Scots law requires no public registration. Since it is a private act, a trust may be latent, that is, unknown to the personal creditors of the truster or the trustees. This creates a risk for anyone extending credit to a trustee since assets which they believe are held as personal patrimony may, in fact, be held in trust for a beneficiary. In any competition between the respective personal rights of a beneficiary and a personal creditor of the trustee, the beneficiary's right will triumph. In principle, this is because the property is part of the trust patrimony and the creditor is a creditor not of the trust estate but of the truster or trustee personally. Moreover, the creditor can choose to protect himself – for example, he could insist on security. Occasionally the law does protect a creditor; for example, a debtor cannot use a trust to evade debts through making a gratuitous alienation (see Chapter 10). Not only is public registration or notification not required: it may not be possible. The delivery of moveable property is usually not recorded in any public register (ships being an exception).

Proposals for reform

The Scottish Law Commission has questioned whether the truster-as-trustee type of trust should remain valid. The concern is the latent trust. If only the beneficiary is aware that assets are held in a trust patrimony, then the trustee's personal creditors may be misled as to his personal credit-worthiness. A possible alternative is to require the written declaration of trust in such a case to be registered in the Books of Council and Session. Given the expense and trouble of doing so, it seems unlikely in future that, as a general rule for the creation of other types of trust, a trust deed will require to be registered.

The Commission has also questioned whether it should remain the law that certain trusts may be constituted other than in writing. It may be, in future, that all trusts must be created using a written declaration of trust, although the writing may not need to be formally valid.

It is also possible that the alternative view of trust creation will be given statutory authority and that the "dual patrimony" theory may also be given parliamentary sanction. There seems to be no desire to turn a trust into a legal person in its own right. Currently, a trust has no separate juristic personality in Scots law.

INVOLUNTARY TRUSTS

It is possible for a trust to be created by implication without a declaration of trust being made voluntarily by a truster. The circumstances in which a trust may arise automatically are defined either under the common law or by statute.

Constructive trusts

The law on constructive trusts is unclear and controversial. A constructive trust is one which arises by operation of law, separately from the will of any truster or trustee. Traditionally, a constructive trust was said to arise in two situations. First, where a person in a fiduciary position (such as a solicitor) unwarrantably gains a personal advantage from that position, the profit they make is regarded as being held in constructive trust for those to whom they owed the fiduciary duty. Second, where a third party to the trust knowingly holds trust property in his possession, having taken it in bad faith, he is sometimes said to hold it in constructive trust for the beneficiaries of the trust. In neither case is there any desire to create a trust and no truster who can be said, even by implication, to have intended to create one: the law simply says that one exists.

The case law on this subject is sparse (*Sutman International* v *Herbage* (1991) may be a relatively unambiguous example). Sometimes, it confuses an implied trust with the usual obligation of a person in a fiduciary position not to abuse the trust reposed in him. The remedy for such an abuse is an action for damages but not every case where a fiduciary position is abused involves a trust in the legal sense. The only circumstance where the courts might need the concept of a constructive trust is where a party injured by another's failure in their fiduciary duty towards him would otherwise lose out to the wrongdoer's creditors. The existence of an implied trust would avoid this because of the rule that a trustee's personal creditors cannot attach the trust fund. However, it would be possible by means of statute to achieve this result by means other than a constructive trust (for example, by granting certain parties a priority in insolvency).

The second category of constructive trust is particularly weak. As Professor Gretton has pointed out, if X has acquired possession of trust property in bad faith, he cannot be a trustee since, to be a trustee, he would have to own the property, not merely possess it (G L Gretton, "Constructive trusts and insolvency"(2000) 3 *European Review of Private Law* 463 at 469).

As a result of the unsatisfactory nature of the law in this area, it is likely to be clarified by statute in future.

Resulting trusts

A resulting trust arises on the failure of the purposes of a private trust where that trust still has assets. The trustees continue to own the property but do so for the benefit of the original truster or his heirs. This arises by implication where the purposes, having failed, can be given no effect and there is no alternative but to return the assets to the truster's estate. Since it is implied, such a reversion can be excluded by the truster either expressly or by implication.

It has been argued that a resulting trust is not a separate kind of trust. Instead, it has been suggested that the law implies in every private trust a rule whereby, if the purposes fail while the trust still has assets, the trustees hold those assets for the truster as the new beneficiary (G L Gretton, "Constructive trusts" (1997) Edin LR 281 at 309–310).

A resulting trust (from the Latin *resultare*, meaning "to spring back") cannot exist if there is some alternative that means the original trust can continue. In public trusts, a possible alternative is the variation of the purposes of the trust at common law or under statute (see Chapter 8).

Fiduciary fees

A fiduciary fee arises where property is granted in liferent and the fee is granted to a person or persons not yet born or not yet ascertained. In other words, property is transferred to X in liferent and (in its most common form) his children in fee. In Scots law, a fee cannot be ownerless and, technically, so long as X was physically able to have more children, the fiars in such a case would be indeterminate. To give effect to the intention of the transferor, however, the courts began to infer that in such an arrangement the liferenter owned the fee as a fiduciary fiar, ie he was effectively holding the fee in trust until a beneficial fiar or fiars emerged. As soon as that happened, and a child was born, the fiduciary fee ends and the fee itself is invested in the fiar, subject to partial defeasance if more fiars (children) emerged. If no beneficial fiar emerged, then the consequence was that the fee became a resulting trust, held for the benefit of the truster.

The fiduciary fee is not a normal kind of trust and there are limitations to the powers of a fiduciary fiar under s 8(2) of the Trusts (Scotland) Act 1921. He must apply to the court to exercise any of the normal powers of a trustee, although he can seek the appointment of an independent trustee to act on behalf of both liferenter and fiar. A fiduciary fiar is, however, subject to the usual duties of a trustee. It is questionable whether the concept of the fiduciary fee really falls into the category of the involuntary creation of a trust. This was a doctrine (no longer of practical relevance in Scots law) which the courts created in order to avoid the legal impossibility of a fee being conveyed to a party that was indeterminate. Arguably, the "truster" all along did intend, and must have intended, to create a voluntary trust in these circumstances.

Essential Facts

- A trust is a tripartite relationship involving one or more trusters, trustees and beneficiaries.
- Traditionally, the creation of trust requires both a declaration of trust by the truster and transfer of trust property to the trustees.

It has been proposed by the Scottish Law Commission that a trust should be created at the point at which a nominated trustee accepts office following the declaration of trust. This would remove any requirement for a transfer of property. The property to be placed in trust would remain vulnerable to the truster's creditors, however, until actually transferred to the trustee or trustees.

- Property which a truster has placed in trust is not available to his personal creditors since it no longer belongs to him. If, as under the alternative theory of trust creation, a trust exists as soon as it is declared, then the truster's creditors may obtain property if they seek to do so before ownership in it is actually transferred to the trustees.

- Property which a trustee holds in trust is not available to his personal creditors since it is owned by him in his capacity as trustee and does not form part of his personal estate.

- A beneficiary has a personal right against the trustees to compel them to carry out the declared trust purposes. This right will prevail over the rights of personal creditors of any of the trustees.

Essential Cases

Barclay's Exr v McLeod (1880): it was the testator's wish and "anxious desire", in leaving his estate to his wife, that she would, after his death, bequeath half of her estate to certain of his relatives. She later died intestate. The court held that the wife's executor need not give effect to her late husband's direction (in effect, his request was merely precatory and no trust purposes had been created).

Sutman International Inc v Herbage (1991): the defenders, while directors of a company, had purchased land in Inverness-shire with funds embezzled from the company and had taken title in their own names. The company was liquidated and an action was brought to have the property transferred to the liquidator. The court held that there was a *prima facie* case for granting the remedy. If the facts were proved, then a clear breach of fiduciary duty would be established in the misappropriation of funds and the property purchased would be regarded as held in constructive trust by the defenders for the company and its liquidator.

3 TRUST PURPOSES

Every trust must have one or more purposes. It is these which express the will of the truster, define the role of the trustees and identify the beneficiaries. The purposes of a trust must be lawful and they must not be impossible, immoral or contrary to public policy. They should not be so vague that trustees could not carry them out, nor so uncertain that beneficiaries could not hold trustees to account for their failure to administer the trust properly.

If a truster specifies no trust purposes – for instance where he conveys trust property to trustees, intending to declare the purposes later but dies before doing so – then the trustees are regarded as holding that property for the benefit of the truster's heir. This is an example of a resulting trust. A "trust for administration" or "bare trust" is one in which no trust purpose is specified except that the trustees should hold an asset in trust for the benefit of one or more beneficiaries.

Trust purposes are usually stated expressly in a trust deed. However, they may also be implied in certain circumstances. A resulting trust is an example of a trust implied by law, the implied purpose being that the trustee holds the property for the benefit of the truster's estate.

UNCERTAINTY

The truster, not the trustee, must define the trust purposes. There is a difference between, on the one hand, giving trustees an element of discretion and, on the other, failing to give them clear directions. For example, a trust may be void from uncertainty when it is not sufficiently clear whom the trustees are to benefit, or how or with what. Uncertainty can arise either because the trust purposes have been expressed in language that is too vague or because they are in themselves simply too wide.

Vagueness

It must be possible to determine the meaning of any purpose laid down by a truster to his trustees. Where the purpose is to promote something which has no determinate meaning, such as the idea of "free thought" in *Hardie* v *Morison* (1899), the court will regard it as void. In this case the truster directed that shop premises be purchased for the sale of books dealing with this subject, but there was no way to determine which books would fall into the class of "free thought" and which would not; therefore it was impossible for the trustees to carry out the instruction. Likewise, the instruction to trustees to dispose of the residue of an estate "in such manner as they may think proper" in *Sutherland's Trs* v *Sutherland's Tr* (1893) was void as a trust purpose. This looked *in effect* like no more than a gift to the trustees, since there was no constraint on how they might choose to dispose of the property and no possibility of their doing so in breach of trust. But it was not a valid gift, since there was no donative intent, and the intended trust was invalid. There was, consequently, a resulting trust in favour of the testator's heirs. As Lord Justice-Clerk Thomson said in *Rintoul's Trs* v *Rintoul* (1949), a testator "cannot leave it to his trustees to make a will for him".

An illustration of the traditional approach of the courts is the case of *Warrender* v *Anderson* (1893). Had the truster in this case directed his trustee to benefit "those who respected me" this would have been invalid, for how was the trustee to identify such persons? On the other hand, a direction to benefit "those whom you know respect me" was held to be valid. The requirement for knowledge on the part of the trustee made this a workable trust purpose because it provided him with a means of defining the beneficiaries. If challenged, of course, the trustee would have had to demonstrate how he knew that the beneficiary had held the truster in respect.

Purposes too wide

It is perfectly competent for trustees to be given the power to select beneficiaries from among a class defined by the truster. However, the class must be defined with sufficient clarity. Otherwise, effect may once again be given to the trustees' purposes rather than the truster's and there is no way of deciding whether the trustees are in breach of trust. The trustees must be given the power to select beneficiaries expressly or by clear implication. Thus, where the truster sought to benefit his "blood relations" in the old case of *Murray* v *Fleming* (1729), this was sufficiently clear since this was a group whose membership could be established. But the purpose of assisting the truster's "relations or other persons" in *Playfair's Trs* v *Playfair* (1900) was too indefinite a description of the class, since it was impossible for any reasonable person to know who the "other persons" were whom the trustee intended to benefit.

Within these two extreme examples, the question of whether a class of beneficiaries can be determined with sufficient precision is a question of degree. There is a difference, for instance, between my "poor relations" or even my "poor friends" (both perhaps being groups whose members trustees may be expected to ascertain) and "poor acquaintances of mine" (a much too vague category): see *Salvesen's Trs* v *Wye* (1954). In general, relationships by blood should be relatively easy to determine. Therefore, for example, the purpose of providing benefit to "the nearest and most needful relatives on my mother's side" has been held to be valid: *Macdonald v Atherton* (1925). Similarly, long-serving past employees of a firm could be left to be identified at the discretion of the trustees: *Hedderwick's Trs v Hedderwick* (1909).

In public trusts, where the truster intends to benefit the public or a section of the public, the class of person who is to receive benefit ought to be reasonably well defined. The courts have been favourable to trusts set up for "charitable purposes". This is a sufficient general intention and, if expressed by the truster, the courts are content to allow trustees to use their discretion to fill in the details of precisely how the trust property should be applied in pursuit of the general purpose: for example, *Turnbull's Trs v Lord Advocate* (1918) and *Hay's Trs v Baillie* (1908). This is in line with the court's general determination not to allow a charitable bequest or trust to be held void for uncertainty, or to fail, if that can possibly be avoided: *Gibson's Trs, Petrs* (1933).

On the other hand, a trust "for religious purposes", according to case law, would be invalid because the purposes are too wide. It is a general purpose to which the courts are not favourable. A trust for religious purposes would give discretion to the trustees to benefit any denomination of any religion, however well established or commonly accepted that religion might be. For example, investing in research to eradicate verticillium wilt in woodlands might be considered a religious purpose by tree worshippers, but is not likely to have been in the mind of most trusters seeking to benefit religion.

It is important not to be confused by the "charity" test in s 7 of the Charities and Trustee Investment (Scotland) Act 2005. The "advancement of religion" is one of the charitable purposes the pursuance of which may justify the registration of a charity in Scotland. However, it will not suffice as a trust purpose. The purposes set out in s 7 deal with registered charities and not trusts: the two are quite separate. Simply because a charity with a certain purpose may be registered as a charity does not mean that it may operate as a trust, since by no means all charities are trusts and not all trusts with charitable purposes are registered charities.

Phrases held by the courts to be too vague (for discussion of which, see W A Wilson and A G M Duncan, *Trusts, Trustees and Executors* (1995), paras 14-73 to 14-90) include "benevolent purposes", "deserving institutions", "public purposes" and "social purposes". On the other hand, "educational purposes" has been regarded as valid, and so has the phrase "philanthropic purposes", being regarded as synonymous with "charitable purposes".

DISJUNCTIVE AND CONJUNCTIVE

Where a list of adjectives is used to describe trust purposes, the court may have to decide whether to interpret that list conjunctively or disjunctively. Did the truster intend the trustees to benefit any of the purposes laid down? If so, then if one purpose is invalid the purposes as a whole must be invalid, otherwise the trustees could apply the trust property exclusively for the invalid purpose. Or did the truster intend that the adjectives qualify the purposes so as to narrow them? If so, the purposes will be valid even if one of the purposes, on its own, would usually be regarded as too wide.

To give an example, suppose that the truster intends to benefit "charitable and religious purposes". There are two possibilities. First, the trustees have discretion to choose one purpose or the other (purpose X *or* purpose Y, read disjunctively). If this is how the provision may be read in the context of the trust deed, and either purpose, charitable or religious, is invalid because it is too wide, then the truster's purposes as a whole are invalid. On a disjunctive reading, therefore, the trust purposes would be void for uncertainty because otherwise the trustees would be free to elect to pursue only (invalid) religious purposes.

The second possibility is that the trustees are to benefit charitable *and* religious purposes (purpose X qualified by purpose Y). In this case the purposes are read conjunctively and will be valid provided that at least one of the purposes is valid. Thus the charitable purposes, which are perfectly valid, are simply qualified by the need also to be religious. It is not "either or"; it is both.

As well as the word "and", it is possible to construe the word "or" in a similar way. The word "or" need not delineate alternatives; it may be used in order that one adjective explain or qualify another. In the context of one trust deed, the phrase "institutions of a benevolent or charitable nature" was held to indicate a valid trust purpose because it was intended to mean one thing, not two: *Hay's Trs* v *Baillie* (1908). The purpose of providing benefit to an institution that was benevolent and charitable was a valid one, whereas the purpose of providing benefit to a benevolent institution, on the one hand, or a charitable one, on the other, was not. Each trust deed must be interpreted in its own terms in order to determine what the truster's intention was.

ADDING SPECIFICITY

A purpose that is too wide may be narrowed by making it more specific. If a provision in favour of religious purposes was narrowed to specify a particular Christian denomination, for example, then it may be valid: *Bannerman's Trs* v *Bannerman* (1915). A mere geographical limitation will not, as a general principle, render valid a purpose that is otherwise invalid. There is a difference between making a bequest for religious purposes in a particular place (this is still a very wide general intention and an invalid purpose) and intending to benefit a particular religious institution (a specific intention and a valid purpose). A direction to do something invalid, albeit in a defined place, cannot readily make the direction more specific and thereby valid. A direction to benefit a class of institution may be too vague. However, if that is narrowed by reference to a particular town or region then a geographical restriction might confer validity: for example *Turnbull's Trs* v *Lord Advocate* (1918).

On the other hand, adding a geographical restriction can add vagueness but, if the purpose is otherwise valid, this addition should not lead to invalidity. An example is the bequest to "charitable institutions connected with the county of Lanark", which was held to be valid in *Cleland's Trs* v *Cleland* (1907). Likewise, when a valid purpose is indicated but the phrase "or for any similar purpose" is added to it, the addition will not invalidate the purpose: *Forrest's Trs* v *Alexander* (1925).

MORALITY

A trust purpose, or a condition attached to such a purpose, will be void if regarded by the court as immoral (*contra bonos mores*). Ideas of morality change over time and the social *mores* of a century ago will not necessarily be those which a court would share in a modern multicultural society. Precedent, particularly in older cases, is therefore a poor guide in this area. Issues in the past have tended to relate to requirements that a beneficiary marry or refrain from doing so; or adhere to, or avoid following, a particular religion. In principle, a trust purpose which required trustees to convey property to a beneficiary only on condition that the beneficiary never married, and undertook never to do so, would be void as *contra bonos mores*. But setting a condition that the beneficiary not marry a specific person, and undertake never to do so, was found to be valid: *Forbes* v *Forbes' Trs* (1882).

The case law in this area is insubstantial and it is questionable how far the courts will be prepared in future to hold trust purpose void on this ground. Although the truster has considerable freedom, in particular when making a testamentary disposition, many would argue that it is not the role of the courts to indulge a truster's personal prejudices unless those prejudices reflect a widespread and generally accepted moral consensus within society.

PUBLIC POLICY

Trust purposes must not be contrary to public policy, although this is again "a varying quantity" (A Mackenzie Stuart, *The Law of Trusts* (1932), p 76). A trust purpose that is wasteful, capricious, extravagant or of no real benefit to anyone falls into this category, as is clear from the *McCaig* cases which dealt with instructions to trustees that costly statues and artistic towers be erected and maintained as memorials to family members: *McCaig* v *University of Glasgow* (1907) and *McCaig's Trs* v *Kirk Session of the United Free Church of Lismore* (1915). While the courts will recognise the right of a truster to provide a memorial of some kind to himself or family members, this must be reasonable and not extravagant: for example, *Aitken's Trs* v *Aitken* (1927). There must be either a public benefit or a patrimonial benefit to a third party. The mere fact that local sculptors might have benefited from the commissions in the *McCaig* cases was seen as merely incidental: fundamentally, the trusts benefited no-one. However, it was recognised that where the person to be memorialised is of historical significance (locally or nationally), then there may be a public benefit (see "Memorials").

PURPOSES SUBJECT TO CONDITIONS

If a trust purpose is valid but is made subject to a condition that is void, then the condition is disregarded (it is held to be *pro non scripto* – as if not written) and effect is given to the purpose. For example, in *Fraser* v *Rose* (1849) the truster in his will provided for his adult daughter on condition that she left her mother within 4 weeks of his death; if she did not cease to cohabit with her, she would forfeit the bulk of the bequest. This condition was held to be void and fell to be disregarded. Since the mother was of good character, the court regarded it as immoral for one parent to attempt to dissolve the obligations which a child has towards the other. Although the condition was void, the bequest itself stood.

As noted, conditions have sometimes been made in regard to marriage. It is a clear rule that it is contrary to public policy for a truster or testator to impose a condition which absolutely prohibits the marriage of a beneficiary (for example, "pay to X, provided that he never marries"). Nor should the beneficiary be placed in a position where, should he choose to marry, he would lose a personal right already vested in him. If the right had not vested – for instance, if the potential beneficiary had married before the death of the truster in a *mortis causa* trust – then a condition excluding him from being a beneficiary would be valid: *Aird's Executors* v *Aird* (1949). In this case, the provision would be "to X at the time of my death, provided he is then unmarried, whom failing, to Y". If X is married at that time then he does not qualify as a beneficiary. The truster's intention need not, in this case, be to prevent X marrying (he could marry and divorce before the truster dies, or marry after the truster's death); rather, it might be to ensure that Y benefits if X is married when the truster dies. Therefore, such a condition is not prohibited on the basis of morality or public policy.

It has been held to be a valid condition to a bequest that a legatee should not marry a particular person ("to X, provided he does not marry Y"). In this case, the bequest was not to be conveyed unless and until a declaration was made by the legatee that he would not marry that person: *Forbes* v *Forbes' Trs* (1882). It is also competent to provide that a beneficiary continue to receive support only while he remains unmarried: *Sturrock* v *Rankin's Trs* (1875).

ILLEGALITY

A trust purpose must not, in itself, be an illegal purpose. That is, it must not require trustees to do something that would be in breach of the criminal law. For example, trustees could not be required, in the fulfilment of a trust purpose, to concern themselves in the sale or supply of controlled drugs in contravention of the Misuse of Drugs Act 1971. If trustees act illegally in the pursuit of a lawful trust purpose, then the trustees may be criminally liable and might, additionally, be liable for breach of trust. This, of course, could have no effect on the trust purpose itself.

A trust purpose that requires trustees to do something that is not competent in law falls to be disregarded. If the purpose itself were lawful and possible, but the trustees were required to carry it out in an unlawful manner, then the purpose would remain valid but the requirement as to its performance would be disregarded.

MEMORIALS

A truster may make provision for the creation and maintenance of a burial place and a memorial to himself or an immediate relative. Such a direction is reasonable even though it confers no benefit on any living person. However, it should not be wasteful or extravagant. In *Aitken's Trs* v *Aitken* (1927) Lord Sands noted the pride of the citizens of Edinburgh in the monument on Princes Street to Sir Walter Scott, but suggested that if a similar monument had been dedicated to some obscure tradesman, whose statue stood in the centre of it, they may have come to regard it as ridiculous. Therefore an extravagant memorial that would inspire ridicule rather than civic pride may be contrary to public policy.

ANIMALS

Lord Sands in *Aitken's Trs* (at 381) also raised the suggestion, *obiter*, that a bequest for the benefit of certain animals may also be reasonable. A trust for the benefit of a class of animals, or the prevention of cruelty to animals in general, will certainly be valid. However, a trust for the benefit of a specified animal or group of animals, such as pets, confers no human or public benefit and the traditional rule is that no such trust can validly be created. According to Mackenzie Stuart (at pp 71–72), the appropriate way of providing for individual animals is to give an annuity to the custodian payable for so long as the animals are living. It has been argued that it is a "natural human sentiment" for a pet owner to wish to make some modest provision for its wellbeing after his death and that such a purpose in a private trust should be valid (K McK Norrie and E M Scobbie, *Trusts* (1991), p 75). However, there is no direct authority for this view.

ENTAILS

It is now unlawful to create a new entail. Historically, the purpose of an entail was to control the succession to heritable property, usually to ensure that it continued in the male line. Thus, if there were no sons, an entailed estate might pass to a brother, nephew or male cousin. The aim was to avoid the usual consequences of heritable succession and to preserve an estate intact, down the generations. In so doing, it would prevent the estate from being split up between co-heiresses or passing into the male line of a son-in-law if, at any time, there should be the absence of a direct male heir. Entails were much criticised in the 18th century and gradually restricted by legislation because of the economic disadvantages they brought. The holder of entailed land could not sell it, or burden it in any way to the prejudice of a subsequent heir of entail. New entails could not be created after 10 August 1914 and all land was finally disentailed by the Abolition of Feudal Tenure (Scotland) Act 2000, ss 50–52.

SUCCESSIVE LIFERENTS

The equivalent of an entail, in respect of moveable property, is a successive liferent (this is a right which can also exist in heritable property but, unlike the entail, has never been restricted to it). It is another example of the attempt to control property from beyond the grave, in this case by creating a mechanism for granting a liferent in property to successive individuals. Like an entail, this could in theory be perpetual and last forever.

Property, heritable or moveable, that was subject to successive liferents could not be sold because it was unmarketable. Rather than being abolished, however, the law seriously restricted successive liferents by s 9 of the Trusts (Scotland) Act 1921 and the law is now found, for deeds executed after 25 November 1968, in s 18 of the Law Reform (Miscellaneous Provisions) (Scotland) Act 1968. This provides that where a person, who was not living or *in utero* at the date of the coming into operation of the deed that created a liferent interest in property, becomes entitled to that interest, then if he is of full age, or when he becomes so, he will own the property absolutely and not hold merely a liferent interest.

Here is an example of what this means. Suppose that in his will Alan grants a liferent interest in trust property (to be administered by nominated trustees) to his daughter, Barbara, and specifies that after Barbara it is to be held by her eldest child, then the eldest child of that child, and so on, in perpetuity. At Alan's death, the will comes into operation. His trustees will own the trust property and Barbara will enjoy a liferent interest. Suppose that Barbara has at that date a daughter, Chloe. Chloe would take the liferent interest after Barbara's death, if she survives her. Chloe's eldest child, however – let us call him David – would, on Chloe's death, become owner of the fee, provided that David had reached the age of 18. (If Chloe died when David was younger than this, then, until reaching 18, the trust would continue and he would only enjoy the liferent until he became 18.) David will become owner of the trust property because he was not alive or *in utero* at the date of Alan's death when the will became effective and the trust was created. Therefore, despite Alan's directions, the law prevents the liferent from continuing beyond David's lifetime. On the other hand, if Chloe had already had David, or was pregnant with him, at the date Alan died, the situation would be different. In that case David would later enjoy only the liferent and his eldest surviving child, provided that he was conceived after Alan's death, would eventually become owner of the fee.

ACCUMULATION OF INCOME

The concept of accumulation of income in a trust is often misunderstood. Where a trust fund generates income, and that income is distributed to beneficiaries, then the income is not being accumulated. The capital may grow, as may the income (for instance, the value of shares may increase and dividends may also increase), but the income is not being accumulated because it is being paid out to beneficiaries. It would be accumulated if, for example, it was used to purchase new shares to be placed into the fund. Therefore it is only where the income from the trust patrimony is re-invested rather than distributed, and the beneficial enjoyment of it is postponed, that accumulation takes place.

Parliament has recognised for centuries that excessive accumulation of income is not in the public interest and could have negative economic effects. In the words of the original legislation used to restrain it, the Accumulations Act 1800, such accumulation "unduly penalises the present generation of potential beneficiaries in order to amass capital for the benefit of a generation to come". Therefore, periods during which the accumulation of trust income may lawfully take place are restricted by legislation. The rules are now contained in s 5 of the Trusts (Scotland) Act 1961, as amended by s 6 of the Law Reform (Miscellaneous Provisions) (Scotland) Act 1966.

Accumulation of income cannot lawfully take place beyond one of the six periods set out below:

(a) the life of the granter;

(b) 21 years from the granter's death;

(c) the minority of any person living or *in utero* at the date of the death of the granter;

(d) the minority of any person who, under the terms of a will or trust deed directing the accumulation, would be entitled, if of full age, to the income directed to be accumulated;

(e) 21 years from the making of the settlement or other disposition (ie the trust deed);

(f) the duration of the minority of any person living or *in utero* at the date of the making of the settlement or other disposition.

These periods are alternatives: it is not possible to add one to another. By "granter" is generally meant the truster or, in the case of a will, the testator. Note that minority is particularly defined, in s 5(6), as the period between birth and the attainment of the age of 21 years. The concept of minority is therefore retained, even though the Age of Legal Capacity (Scotland) Act 1991 has largely removed it from other areas of Scots law.

Any accumulation which is directed for a period other than one of those above is void. However, that does not mean the trust deed is void: only that the *excess* period of accumulation is void. Any income accumulated contrary to s 5 must go to the person or persons who would have been entitled to it had the unlawful accumulation not been directed (s 5(3)). In other words, the court will select and apply one of the periods above in order to determine the appropriate period of accumulation that should have applied, and then order the income accumulated beyond that period to be distributed to the appropriate beneficiaries.

CHOICE OF ACCUMULATION PERIOD

How should the court select the appropriate period of accumulation? It will not necessarily seek to apply the period it thinks the testator would have intended. The testator in these circumstances probably never considered that the period of accumulation he originally intended was unlawful. It may attempt to determine when accumulation was to begin: if it was to begin during the lifetime of the truster, then the choice is restricted to (a), (d), (e) or (f). Without express reference to the minority of a beneficiary, it seems unlikely that (c), (d) or (f) could apply. Wilson and Duncan (para 9.39) suggest that period (e) will apply in most *inter vivos* trusts, unless reference is made to the period of the truster's life, in which case (a) would obviously apply.

Sometimes the period to be selected is fairly obvious, as, for instance, where accumulation is directed to commence on the death of the truster (wherein (b) would apply). But accumulation might be directed to begin on the happening of some other event, for instance the termination of a liferent. The truster, expecting the liferenter to die leaving a child under the age of 21, may direct that the income be accumulated for the benefit of that child from the date of death of the liferenter. Of course, during the currency of the liferent nothing is accumulated since any income is being paid to the liferenter. After the liferenter dies, assuming that the child is under 21, accumulation of income would take place until the child's 21st birthday: this is a result of period (d) above. In this example, the accumulation period would almost certainly be less than 21 years. In fact, if the beneficiary were already of "full age" (ie 21) when the liferenter died, there could be no accumulation at all since he would be immediately entitled to the income.

The rules regarding accumulation have been criticised by the Scottish Law Commission as being complex and anachronistic (Scot Law Com No 142 (2010), paras 5.6–5.7). The Commission has proposed granting jurisdiction to the Court of Session to vary the purposes of long-term private trusts after a period of time (25 years has been suggested), in order to take account of any material change of circumstances (para 5.57). In making a variation, the court would have regard to the truster's intentions, where possible, or the probable intentions of a reasonable truster in the current circumstances of the trust.

Essential Facts

- Trust purposes must be lawful and must not be impossible, immoral or contrary to public policy.
- Vague trust purposes are not valid because they would grant too much discretion to trustees, effectively allowing them to pursue their own purposes at the risk of turning an obligation of trust into a donation of trust property to trustees.
- Trusts and registered charities must be distinguished. The law treats trusts for charitable purposes favourably but a trust for religious purposes will be invalid unless some qualification is made in order to narrow those purposes.
- The court's construction of trust purposes will depend on the context of each individual trust deed and the importance of interpretative context means that prior decided cases may provide only limited assistance.
- Attempts to control property in perpetuity from beyond the grave, by the use of entails and successive liferents, have been prohibited or restricted by Parliament.
- The law restricts, within defined statutory limits, the accumulation of income by trustees; that is, the re-investment of income from trust property into the trust patrimony. An invalid period of accumulation will be replaced by the courts with a valid one and income unlawfully accumulated within the trust patrimony will be directed to be paid to those beneficiaries who would have been entitled to it had the appropriate lawful period of accumulation been directed by the truster.

Essential Cases

McCaig v University of Glasgow (1907): a testator sought to leave property in trust for the building of "artistic towers" on his estates, together with statues of his parents and children. He stated his desire to encourage young artists and prizes were to be given for the best plans for these constructions. The court held that the trust was invalid because of the rule of disinherison. That is, the testator could not disinherit his heir-at-law (the testator's sister) without conferring a beneficial right to his property on someone else. Since this had not been done, the heir had not been divested successfully.

McCaig's Trs v Kirk Session of the United Free Church of Lismore (1915): the heir in the first *McCaig* case purported to leave her property in trust. The trustees were to maintain a circular tower in Oban which her brother had built and to have statues of her parents and siblings made and installed there, with the building then to be sealed and to be kept private. The sister had no heirs. The court held that the bequest was contrary to public policy since, in its degree and scale, it involved a sheer waste of money in the pursuit of the testator's vanity. The fact that it might afford employment to sculptors did not save the bequest since it was, in itself, unreasonable and the intention was not to benefit those who would have carried out the work. In this, as in the previous *McCaig* case, the judges took the view that if the work were carried out it would not represent a lasting memorial but would become the subject of ridicule. The court acknowledged that there was a clear difference between what a person might do in their own lifetime, if they so chose, however unreasonable it might be, and what they might make the subject of a bequest.

Aitken's Trs v Aitken (1927): the testator, one of the last of a family connected for centuries to the town of Musselburgh, who had twice been elected as champion at the riding of the marches, desired in his will that a massive equestrian bronze statue of himself, as champion, be erected in memory of his family and himself on a site on a main street. The Inner House of the Court of Session held that the directions were invalid as being contrary to public policy. Although the object of creating a memorial was seen as rational and reasonable, the town council had not supported the idea and Lord Sands regarded the directions as a whole as "an irrational, futile, and self-destructive scheme to carry out not unreasonable purposes". No benefit would be conferred on the town or its citizens.

Aird's Exrs v Aird (1949): a testator bequeathed his estate to his brother so long as he remained a single man. If the brother married, the estate was to go elsewhere. The brother married in 1906 and the testator died in 1947. The court held that the brother was not entitled to the bequest. The testator intended to benefit his brother if he was unmarried and others if he was. Since the brother did not meet the condition of being unmarried, he did not take the legacy.

Carey's Trs v Rose (1957): a testator directed his trustees to hold the residue of his estate in trust for the legitimate son of his nephew, R, "who shall first attain the age of 21 years", with a destination over in favour of other heirs. He gave no directions in regard to the income of the residue. R, who eventually became entitled to the residue, was born 2 years after the death of the testator and the trustees had to accumulate the income for a period of 23 years. The court held that, by implication, accumulation had been directed to take place from the testator's date of death and that income accumulated during any period after 21 years from that date must fall into intestacy.

4 THE APPOINTMENT OF TRUSTEES

A trust cannot function without one or more trustees to administer it. A truster will usually nominate trustees in a trust deed. The choice of potential nominees is circumscribed by the requirement that a trustee have the legal capacity to hold office. A person under the age of 16, as a general rule, lacks such capacity by virtue of s 1(1) and (2) of the Age of Legal Capacity (Scotland) Act 1991. Under s 3 of this Act, persons aged 16 or 17 may have "prejudicial transactions" involving them set aside provided that they apply to do so before reaching the age of 21. This remedy is not available in certain circumstances – for instance, where the transaction was ratified by the court at the time; or where it was ratified by the applicant after he attained the age of 18; or where the applicant, through fraud, induced the other party to enter into the transaction (see, further, W A Wilson and A G M Duncan, *Trusts, Trustees and Executors* (1995), paras 18-06 to 18-12). Given the potential problems that may arise, it is advisable for a truster not to nominate a person under the age of 18 as a trustee.

WHO MAY ACT AS A TRUSTEE?

A person who is a foreign national (except an enemy alien) can act as a trustee, as can a person who resides abroad, although such a person may be subject to removal, at the discretion of the court, under s 23 of the Trusts (Scotland) Act 1921. Obviously, a person who is *incapax* by reason of insanity cannot accept office as a trustee. Any trustee who loses the mental capacity to function in that office may also be removed under s 23 of the 1921 Act.

A trustee may be a juristic person. A corporate body can therefore act as a trustee, provided that it is competent to do so in terms of its constitution. A public body, such as a local authority, also has the capacity to act as a trustee, usually with the relevant local authority administrative office-bearers for the time being acting as trustees.

ORIGINAL TRUSTEES

The truster, when creating the trust, will generally nominate those who are to be its trustees. Until they accept office (and they are free to decline), they remain merely nominees. Once they have accepted office, provided that they have the requisite legal capacity to act, they become what is called "original trustees". Those who become trustees later are called "assumed trustees". There is no legally prescribed form of nomination of original trustees. They need not be specifically named in order to be nominated: it is enough that they are clearly identified. Nominating, for example, "the same trustees as my brother" would be sufficient: *Martin* v *Ferguson's Trs* (1892). It is open to a truster to nominate trustees to be appointed by some third party.

The truster may appoint a trustee *sine qua non*. Such a trustee, if he accepts, has a right of veto over the acts of his co-trustees. In other words, if the trustee *sine qua non* does not vote in favour of a decision, even if the majority of trustees are in favour, the decision will be invalid.

THE POWER OF THE TRUSTER TO NOMINATE TRUSTEES

In a private trust, it is implied under the common law that a truster retains the power to nominate new trustees on the failure of the original or assumed trustees. Therefore, while the truster survives, an *inter vivos* trust should never lack trustees, since the truster retains the right to appoint new ones. This is not the case in public trusts, however, since on the failure of such a trust, including failure caused by lack of trustees, only the court may appoint new trustees (see, below, "Appointment by the court").

EX OFFICIO TRUSTEES

The truster may nominate an *ex officio* trustee. That is, rather than nominate an individual by name, an office-holder is nominated (such as a treasurer or council member), so that whoever holds the office for the time being will act as a trustee. Usually, a truster identifies the particular characteristics of an individual that qualifies him, at least in the truster's opinion, to act as a suitable trustee (*delectus personae*). In the case of an *ex officio* trustee, however, the truster identifies the general qualities required for anyone who is appointed to a particular office as being suitable also for carrying on the role of trustee. This is particularly common in clubs, where the secretary or treasurer, for example, may be trustees *ex officio* . Historically, it has also been common in local church organisations, where ministers or parish clerks might be nominated.

This raises the question of whether it is possible to accept an office but refuse to be assumed as an *ex officio* trustee. The answer depends on whether being a trustee is intrinsic to holding the office. If a truster nominates as an *ex officio* trustee a member of a local council, for example, then, since being a councillor is completely separate from being a trustee, it is open to the councillor to decline the latter office. On the other hand, if no-one can be treasurer of the bowling club without taking on, *ex officio*, the role of trustee, then it is impossible to hold one of these offices without holding the other. Agreeing to act as a trustee may, therefore, be a pre-condition of accepting an office, although, of course, no *ex officio* trustee can be forced to accept office against his will: for example, *Vestry of St Silas Church* v *Trs of St Silas Church* (1945). Once a person accepts office as an *ex officio* trustee, if he subsequently loses or resigns from the office he will also cease to be a trustee.

It may be the case that an office is not automatically linked to the role of trustee. This would arise where the trust deed specified that some personal characteristic of the trustee was relevant and it was not the case that whoever happened to hold the office for the time being would suffice as a trustee. For example, a particular office may be open to any member of the legal profession. However, if the trust deed specified that only holders of that office who were also Writers to the Signet may act as trustees, then the intention of the truster would have to be respected.

The truster's intention is also relevant where the office changes in character in some fundamental way; for instance, if the office amalgamated with another. The truster has chosen the holder of a particular office to be one of his trustees because of some quality intrinsic to that office; if the office should change so that its character is fundamentally different, then that intention may be frustrated and the nomination of the office-holder may become invalid. This is a question of circumstances: for example, *Mailler's Trs* v *Allan* (1904).

ASSUMED TRUSTEES

Unless otherwise stated in the trust deed, under s 3(b) of the Trusts (Scotland) Act 1921 the trustee or trustees in all trusts have the power to assume "new trustees". This includes the power to assume only one new trustee: *Kennedy, Petr* (1983). The trustees may assume any person they choose to be a new trustee, but if the truster had specified in the trust deed a particular qualification or characteristic – for instance that trustees must have the surname Smith; or a degree in physics; or that X is to be assumed when he reaches the age of 25 years – then that would be binding. Moreover, the trustees have a duty of care to the beneficiaries in the selection of any new trustee. This means that they should not select any person obviously unfit for the office.

It is rare for a truster to exclude the operation of s 3(b). Such a restriction may validly restrict the power to assume by reserving it to particular trustees or in some other way imposing a condition upon its use. Where the use of the power to assume is conditional, and the condition cannot be met, then the Court of Session in the exercise of its *nobile officium* may be able to provide a remedy by authorising the assumption of new trustees and varying or removing the condition: for example, *Adamson's Trs, Petrs* (1917). An *ex officio* trustee may assume new *ex officio* trustees under s 3(b): *Winning, Petrs* (1999).

APPOINTMENT BY THE COURT

Even if all the nominated trustees decline office, the trust will usually survive. In an *inter vivos* trust, provided it is a private trust, the truster has an inherent right at common law to nominate alternative trustees. If the truster is unable to exercise this right (for example, through having become *incapax*) or, in the case of a *mortis causa* trust, the court has the power to appoint trustees, either at common law or under s 22 of the Trusts (Scotland) Act 1921. In a public trust, once the trust has taken effect, the appointment of new trustees is a matter for the court, either in a petition under s 22 or in the exercise of the *nobile officium* of the Court of Session, unless the truster expressly reserved in the trust deed the power to appoint alternative trustees in the event that the all the original trustees declined office.

Under s 22 of the 1921 Act, the Court of Session or an appropriate sheriff court may appoint a trustee or trustees under a deed of trust in the following circumstances:

- when the trustees cannot be assumed under the trust deed (for example, there are no surviving trustees and the truster is *incapax*); or
- when a sole trustee is or has become insane or incapable of acting by reason of physical or mental disability, or by being continuously absent from the United Kingdom for at least 6 months or by having disappeared for at least 6 months.

The common law power to appoint trustees will only be used in circumstances where s 22 does not apply. These include circumstances where a sole trustee is removed due to unsatisfactory conduct, where the office of an *ex officio* trustee is abolished, or where the trustees are deadlocked and it is necessary to resolve this by assuming a new trustee: *Aikman, Petr* (1881).

The Scottish Law Commission has proposed simplifying the law in this area and replacing s 22 (Scot Law Com No 126 (2004), para 4.8). The proposal is that the court should have power, on the application of a trustee or any person with an interest in the trust estate, to appoint a trustee where this is necessary for the administration of the trust.

ACCEPTANCE OF OFFICE

No-one acts as a trustee usually unless he has voluntarily accepted office. However, there is no prescribed form for doing so, and acceptance of office may be express or implied. As Mackenzie Stuart (*The Law of Trusts* (1932), p 154) put it, acceptance of office "will usually be inferred if the person alleged to be trustee has performed the usual duties of a trustee, either personally or by directing others". Of course, the person must be aware of his nomination before any such inference can be drawn. For the avoidance of doubt, it is advisable for a trustee to accept or decline office in writing.

There are two circumstances where acceptance arises automatically. First, as noted above, becoming a trustee may be a condition of accepting office in a club or other voluntary organisation. The acceptance is still voluntary, but in these circumstances it may be the case that there is no possibility of holding the office without also being a trustee. Second, a person may be deemed to have become a trustee by operation of law. This would be both automatic and involuntary.

The nomination of trustees is usually joint and several. That means that where several trustees are nominated, the fact that one, or more than one, decline(s) office will not prejudice the right of the remaining nominees to accept office. In the highly unusual event that the nomination is joint, however, then the declinature of one vitiates the nomination of the others.

The consequence of accepting office is that a personal right to the trust estate is vested in the trustee or trustees and they have a duty to turn this into a real right (known as "completing title"). There is no difference in the powers of an original trustee and those of an assumed trustee and the same considerations apply to both in terms of accepting office. When exercising the power of assumption, trustees may use a particular style of deed of assumption and conveyance found in Sch B to the Trusts (Scotland) Act 1921 in order to complete title. This ensures that the trust property is conveyed to the assumed trustees so that the property is held jointly by all of the trustees, whether new or subsisting trustees.

If the truster appoints a trustee *sine qua non* who declines to accept office, it is presumed that the trust is created according to the usual rules of trust creation. Of course, it is open to the truster to direct that the existence of the trust depends on acceptance by a specific nominated trustee.

RESIGNATION

Unless the trust deed specifies otherwise, and with the exception of a sole trustee, every gratuitous trustee has the power to resign the office of trustee: s 3(a) of the Trusts (Scotland) Act 1921. A sole trustee, under s 3(a) and proviso (1) of that Act, may not resign unless he has assumed one or more new trustees, and they have accepted office, or the court has appointed new trustees or a judicial factor. Where a sole trustee does resign and assumes a trustee as a replacement, there is a particular duty to exercise reasonable care in the selection of the new trustee.

A trustee who accepts any legacy or bequest given to him on condition that he accepts the office of trustee is not entitled to resign unless the trust deed says so. The same is true of any trustee appointed on the basis that he shall be remunerated for serving as a trustee. In both cases, the trust deed must specifically grant a power to resign, although the court may grant a trustee authority to resign under s 3 of the Trusts (Scotland) Act 1921.

A trustee who resigns is divested of the trust property which automatically, without conveyance, accrues to the remaining trustees: s 20 of the 1921 Act. This is a consequence of the fact that trust property is joint property.

Resignation, it seems, must be carried out expressly and in writing. Schedule A to the 1921 Act contains the form of a minute of resignation which will take effect, under s 19, when intimated to all the other trustees; it should then be registered in the Books of Council and Session. A trustee should be careful to give notice of his resignation to interested third parties or risk future liability. In regard to beneficiaries, resignation absolves the trustee from future liability in any question with them.

DEATH

Obviously, a trustee who dies ceases to be a trustee. His heirs or executors do not replace him (unless the trust deed specifies otherwise). Since trust property is joint property (which is indivisible), the deceased trustee held no separate share in it. Instead, the remaining trustees simply become joint owners of the property without any need for a conveyance. This is because of an implied survivorship: if one trustee dies, ownership of the trust property remains with the surviving trustees. There is no need to intimate the death of a trustee to the other trustees since death is regarded as a public fact.

As a consequence of the death of a trustee, his representatives may seek a formal discharge of liability from the surviving trustees. A resigning trustee may do the same. If the trustees refuse to grant such a discharge, the beneficiaries may do so and, if they also refuse or are unable to grant one, the court may grant a judicial discharge under s 18 of the Trusts (Scotland) Act 1921.

REMOVAL OF TRUSTEES

The Court of Session under its *nobile officium* has a power to remove a trustee where this is necessary for the proper administration of the trust. Persistent conduct in prejudice of the administration of the trust will justify removal; as may a situation where a trustee finds himself personally in a position where he cannot act as a trustee impartially, or without conflict of interest. Minor irregularities, such as minor acts of carelessness, will not justify removal. A serious breach of trust in the form of embezzlement will certainly lead to removal: *Wishart, Petrs* (1910).

The common law power subsists even though grounds now exist under s 23 of the Trusts (Scotland) Act 1921 to remove a trustee. These are that the trustee:

(a) is or has become insane; or
(b) is or has become incapable of acting by reason of mental or physical disability; or
(c) has been continuously absent from the United Kingdom for at least 6 months; or
(d) has disappeared for at least 6 months.

Where ground (a) or (b) is established, the court *must* grant the application for removal. The court has discretion in regard to grounds (c) and (d). Ground (c) is generally recognised as outdated, having been drafted in an age when instantaneous communication across the world was not as readily available as it is today, and the court is not likely to remove a trustee on this ground merely on the basis of absence without evidence that this is actually obstructing the administration of the trust.

Under the present law it is only the court which has discretionary power to remove a trustee, having received an application to do so from a co-trustee, beneficiary or other person with an interest. Even if all the beneficiaries agree that it would be preferable for a trustee to be removed, the court retains its discretion and is not bound to remove the trustee: *McWhirter* v *Latta* (1889).

The Scottish Law Commission has proposed significant reform in this area. The Commission favours giving a general statutory power to the court to remove a trustee which will replace the current statutory power and the common law power. It has suggested (Discussion Paper on Trustees and Trust Administration (Scot Law Com No 126, 2004), para 4.38) that the court be given the power to remove a trustee if it is satisfied that (a) the trustee is unfit or unable to continue to act as trustee in the trust; or (b) the trustee has neglected his duties as trustee. An application to this end might be brought by one of the trustees, any beneficiary or any other person with an interest in the trust estate.

While rejecting the possibility of allowing beneficiaries the direct power to remove a trustee or to have removal become the automatic consequence of specific events, such as incapacity or bankruptcy, the Commission has proposed that trustees be given discretionary power to remove one of their number. This power would be exercisable on their becoming aware that a trustee is certified as being mentally incapable of acting as a trustee or has been imprisoned or convicted of a crime involving dishonesty. Where there were more than two trustees, a deed executed by a majority of the trustees (not counting the one to be removed) would be necessary. If there were two trustees, one could remove the other if a ground were established.

Essential Facts

- A trustee may be a natural or a juristic person and may hold office *ex officio*.
- Trustees may be original (nominated by the truster) or assumed (nominated by existing trustees) or appointed by the courts in certain circumstances.
- Trustees must accept office, but can do so expressly or impliedly, and, having done so, gain the right to complete title to the trust property.
- By default, trustees have the power to resign, with the exception of sole trustees who must first assume new trustees.
- Trustees can be removed only by the court which has common law and statutory grounds for ordering such removal; this area of law may be reformed to grant the majority of trustees a power of removal.

Essential Cases

Mailler's Trs v Allan (1904): a minister of the United Presbyterian Church appointed certain trustees to hold and administer
the residue of his estate. Among them were, *ex officio*, ministers
of churches in the United Presbyterian Church and their successors. In 1900 the United Free Church was created following the
union of the United Presbyterian Church and a majority in the Free
Church. The *ex officio* trustees petitioned for authority to continue
to act as trustees. The court held that the ministers of the churches
named by the truster, now belonging to the United Free Church,
and their successors, were entitled to act as trustees because the *ex
officio* trustees had not varied their principles or done anything to
render the carrying out of the trust impossible in accordance with
the desires of the truster. The amalgamation of the churches did not
make a fundamental difference to their position.

Adamson's Trs, Petrs (1917): under a marriage contract the
trustees had the power to assume new trustees with the consent of
the spouses. The wife having become insane, with no prospect of
recovery, the court, in the exercise of its *nobile officium*, authorised
the trustees to assume new trustees without her consent.

McWhirter v Latta (1889): the testator created a trust in favour
of his wife as liferentrix of the residue of his estate and his issue
as fiars. A single trustee was appointed. All the beneficiaries petitioned for removal of the trustee and the appointment of a judicial
factor, on the ground that the trustee, who was on bad terms with
the liferentrix, unjustifiably interfered with her enjoyment of the
liferent. The court held that he should be removed. Moral delin-
quency or malversation was not necessary to remove a trustee: a
breach of trust, even from error of judgement, may suffice. In this
case the trustee sought to administer the estate without consulting
the liferentrix, and by his behaviour had created deadlock in terms
of the trust administration, therefore he had to be removed.

Vestry of St Silas Church v Trustees of St Silas Church (1945): a
truster bequeathed a sum to the "trustees patrons and vestrymen" of
an English Episcopal church in Glasgow. This was to be held by them,
and their successors in office, as trustees as a fund for augmenting

the stipend of the incumbent of that church. After the truster died, the church changed its constitution. Trustees and patrons were appointed by assumption, whereas vestrymen were to be elected by the congregation and two of them were to retire annually. Elected vestrymen did not automatically become trustees of the augmentation fund, and had to agree to be assumed, while the trustees and patrons could themselves be assumed without necessarily becoming trustees of the fund. No elected vestryman was thereafter assumed as a trustee and it was argued that a candidate for office of vestryman should, under the amended constitution, be taken to have declined the office of trustee of the augmentation fund. The court held that the pursuers were entitled, as vestrymen, to act as trustees if they agreed to do so. They were the successors in office of the vestrymen appointed under the original constitution, and although the mode of appointment had changed this was not so fundamental as to affect their qualification to act as *ex officio* trustees.

5 THE ADMINISTRATION OF TRUSTS

THE POWERS OF TRUSTEES

Trustees originally derived their powers exclusively from the trust deed. This is now rare, since Parliament, in s 4 of the Trusts (Scotland) Act 1921, has created implied powers for trustees which exist by default unless they are excluded by, or incompatible with, the express terms of the trust deed. The Court of Session, in the exercise of its *nobile officium*, can also grant specific powers to trustees by way of equitable remedy.

Since trustees are owners of trust property, it is slightly artificial to refer to their "powers", although that is how they are conventionally described. Where owners of property are concerned, usually they are said to have rights in relation to their property, such as the right of sale. This is merely a point of terminology but it masks the fact that trustees, as owners of the trust patrimony, are only restricted from acting, like other owners, by the general law or under the law of obligations (K G C Reid, *The Law of Property in Scotland* (1996), para 691).

THE DEED OF TRUST

Every trust deed is different and it is always necessary for the court to interpret the provisions of individual deeds in order to ascertain what powers the trustees have. The truster may decide to nominate one or more trustees *sine qua non,* that is, trustees who must agree to any act of trust administration for it to be valid. Such a trustee effectively has a veto in respect of any trust decision, although such appointments are now rare. Likewise, the truster may require all trustees to act jointly. This means that all the trustees must unanimously agree to each act of trust administration. Such provisions are also rare in practice. Usually, a quorum of trustees can make valid decisions.

GENERAL POWERS OF TRUSTEES UNDER S 4 OF THE 1921 ACT

Unless at variance with the "terms or purposes" of the trust, trustees are deemed to hold a range of powers set out in s 4. These include (but are not limited to) the following powers:

- to sell the trust estate (whether heritable or moveable);
- to grant leases of heritable estate and to remove tenants;
- to borrow money on the security of any part of the trust estate;
- to excamb (exchange) any heritable estate that is trust property;
- to make any kind of investment;
- to purchase heritable property for any purpose;
- to appoint and remunerate factors and law agents;
- to discharge trustees who have resigned or the representatives of any who have died;
- to uplift, discharge or assign debts due to the trust;
- to enter into arbitration;
- to write off debts they reasonably deem irrecoverable;
- to grant all deeds necessary for exercising their powers.

Note that trustees do not have the power to grant servitudes over trust property unless the trust deed states or implies that they have.

PROTECTION OF TITLE FOR *INTRA VIRES* BREACH OF TRUST

Where the trustees use any of the first six of the implied powers listed above to enter into a transaction with a third party, the validity of that transaction will not be challengeable by anyone on the ground that "the act in question is at variance with the terms or purposes of the trust": Trusts (Scotland) Act 1961, s 2(1). Good faith is irrelevant. This means, for example, that if the trustees sell trust property to a third party, the third party's title cannot be challenged on the ground that, in fact, the trustees lacked the power to sell. This is true even if the third party was aware that there was no power to sell. Section 2(1) does not mean that trustees are free from liability to co-trustees or beneficiaries: it is simply about title. If the trustees, in breach of trust, make a gift of trust property to a third party then the gift will be voidable since power to donate is not implied by s 4 nor is it one of the six powers referred to in s 2(1).

ADDITIONAL POWERS GRANTED BY THE COURT UNDER STATUTORY AUTHORITY

Section 5 of the Trusts (Scotland) Act 1921 permits the court, on the petition of the trustees under any trust (public or private), to grant them authority to exercise any of the general powers listed in s 4, notwithstanding that this may be at variance with the terms or purposes of the trust. The court can do so only if satisfied that the act the trustees wish to perform is in all the circumstances expedient for the execution of the trust.

This section had greater scope for application before the 1921 Act was amended to include the power to sell heritage as one of the general powers under s 4. It will be quite rare for the test of expediency not to be met by the trustees in their petition. A petition under s 5 may sometimes be brought in the context of a re-organisation of the trust and variation of its purposes (on variation, see Chapter 8). *Inverclyde Council* v *Dunlop* (2005) was a case of this kind, in which the terms of a public trust set up to preserve a park for the use of the public required to be varied. The trustees lacked the funds to maintain a pavilion on the park and they wanted to build and lease out a gym that would raise funds to meet the original purposes of the trust. A power in the trust deed to let existing residential cottages in the park, in order to defray running costs, did not include any power to let other areas of the park and the power to levy charges for entry was restricted. The court held that the test of expediency justifying the extension of these powers had been made out.

ADDITIONAL POWERS GRANTED UNDER THE COMMON LAW

The Court of Session, through the exercise of its *nobile officium*, has discretion to grant trustees authority to do acts which otherwise they lack the power to do. Since this is a jurisdiction to grant an equitable remedy where no other remedy exists, it cannot be used if an application under s 5 of the 1921 Act is available to the trustees. Moreover, since it is an interference with the truster's autonomy, it will be exercised rarely and generally in order to allow effect to be given to the purposes of the trust where this would otherwise become impossible. For compelling reasons, and again only in exceptional circumstances, the court may use this power to sanction an *ultra vires* breach of trust by trustees who have purported to exercise powers they did not have: for example, *Dow's Trs* (1947).

THE POWER TO ADVANCE CAPITAL

When the income from a trust fund is inadequate to meet the trust purposes the court, under s 16 of the Trusts (Scotland) Act 1921, has the power to authorise trustees to advance capital from the trust fund to beneficiaries under the age of 18 where this is not prohibited under the trust deed. This power is a narrow one based on the following conditions. First, the advance must be necessary for the education or maintenance of any beneficiary under that age. Although the order must be made while the beneficiary is under 18, advances of capital can continue to be made after the beneficiary reaches that age (provided that they are made in furtherance of trust purposes). Second, the beneficiary concerned must have either a vested or a contingent right in the capital. If the right is contingent, it must depend only upon the beneficiary's survival. For instance, the condition may be that the beneficiary will gain a vested right to the capital only if and when he reaches the age of 21. Vesting contingent on another kind of uncertain event, such as university graduation, would not be a foundation for an advance of capital.

At common law, under the *nobile officium*, the Court of Session has equitable power to grant advances of capital but this is still subject to the condition that the advance must be necessary for the education or maintenance of a beneficiary. This power can be exercised only where the statutory power is incompetent and it may be exercised to provide a remedy only where there is some unforeseen circumstance for which the truster has made no provision, resulting in no or inadequate provision for the education and maintenance of his children. However, the power is not limited to beneficiaries aged under 18 and it is not necessary for the beneficiary to have a vested right in the estate. An order may be made, therefore, to make an advance to an adult. Usually such an advance will be deducted from the share of the truster's property to which the beneficiary would eventually be entitled.

The Scottish Law Commission (Discussion Paper on *Trustees and Trust Administration* (Scot Law Com 126, 2004), para 6.19; revised in Discussion Paper on *Supplementary and Miscellaneous Issues relating to Trust Law* (Scot Law Com No 148, 2011), para 9.15) has proposed reform in order to replace s 16 and the common law power with a new statutory provision that would apply where the truster did not prohibit in the trust deed the advancement of capital. This would grant trustees the default power to advance up to half of a beneficiary's share in the capital of the trust fund provided that every person with a prior interest in the trust estate, who might be prejudiced, consented. At the date an advance was made, the beneficiary would need to have a vested right to the capital (which might be subject to defeasance) or a right which would vest on the occurrence of some uncertain future event. If a person who may be prejudiced refused to consent, the court would have power to authorise an advance where that consent was unreasonably withheld. Similarly, if such a person lacked capacity to consent, the court may authorise an advance on their behalf. The trustees would also have the power to impose conditions on the payment of the advance.

TAKING DECISIONS

What the truster states in the trust deed has precedence in determining precisely how decisions will be validly taken in the administration of the trust. However, usually, decision-making is by quorum and the default position, under s 3(c) of the 1921 Act, is that a quorum is the majority of the accepting and surviving trustees. Where there are two trustees, a quorum will always be two.

Assuming that the quorum is the majority, this does not mean that the majority present at any meeting can make a valid decision. It means the majority of all the surviving trustees must do so. Therefore if three out of five trustees constitute the quorum and, at a meeting, these three agree to a decision, then the decision is validly taken. If the majority of those present (ie two of the three) agree, this is not a quorum of the surviving trustees therefore the decision is not valid.

There are two additional points to note here. First, any trustee with a personal interest in the outcome of the decision does not count (unless the trust deed specifies otherwise). Therefore, if the quorum is a majority of trustees, this means the majority of those not disqualified from acting due to a personal interest. For example, if two of six trustees are disqualified, then a valid decision may be made by only three trustees even though, usually, a quorum would be four. Second, if a minority of trustees dissent from a decision, they remain equally liable for the decision with those who voted in favour. This is because all trustees are regarded, when they accept office, as impliedly agreeing to abide by majority decision. A dissenting trustee who is part of the minority might be able to exercise the power to resign, or may seek interdict if he believes that the decision represents a breach of trust. Otherwise, that trustee is bound to implement the decision: for example, *Lynedoch* v *Outcherlony* (1827).

The Scottish Law Commission has also proposed replacing s 3(c) of the 1921 Act, in order to remove the concept of a "quorum" (Scot Law Com No 126 (2004), para 2.22). It suggests a rule whereby a decision will bind all trustees if it is taken by a number amounting to at least the majority of the trustees then acting and qualified to vote. Obviously, any trustee with a personal interest will not be qualified to vote. This default rule would be overridden by any contrary provision in a trust deed.

MEETINGS

The idea of a quorum suggests a physical meeting of the trustees. In fact, a physical meeting is not regarded in practice as necessary, provided that each trustee has an opportunity to contribute on an informed basis to making the decision. The law is not entirely clear on whether trustees are required to hold a physical meeting. The Scottish Law Commission wishes to add clarity by proposing legislation. This would enact that, unless a trust deed provided otherwise, a binding decision could only be made if all the trustees, so far as is reasonably practicable, had been given adequate prior notice of the matters to be decided and an opportunity to put forward their views, either by attending a meeting of the trustees or in any other manner (Scot Law Com No 126 (2004), para 2.11).

CONSULTATION

When it comes to making a decision, all trustees have a right to be consulted. This right is not absolute: there may be special circumstances where a decision must be taken suddenly and a trustee cannot be contacted, or is temporarily unable to participate. All trustees must be given a reasonable opportunity to participate in making decisions and, if they are not, then any decision made will be invalid: for example *Wyse* v *Abbott* (1881).

While trustees are under no absolute obligation to participate in decision-making (since the failure of any one trustee to do so will not usually invalidate a decision), there is an expectation that they will all do so. The underlying idea is that trustees should meet to deliberate so that the benefit of their combined experience can be brought to bear on the administration of the trust. After all, that is why they were appointed. The "unreasonable or wilful refusal to perform the duties of the office" will justify a trustee's removal by the court: *MacGilchrist's Trs* v *MacGilchrist* (1930), per Lord Morison.

The court in the case of *Malcolm* v *Goldie* (1895) took the view that it was "a mere futile formality" for a quorum of trustees to give notice of a meeting to a trustee who had moved to Australia, with no intention of returning to Scotland, since that trustee would not in any event have attended the meeting. However, with modern communications, mere residence abroad is no longer a practical ground for removing trustees or not making reasonable efforts to consult them. The court still has the power, under s 23 of the 1921 Act, to remove any trustee who has been continuously absent from the UK for 6 months or more, but is unlikely to exercise it unless the trustee has in some way intentionally cut himself off from participating in the administration of the trust.

INTERFERENCE WITH THE DISCRETION OF THE TRUSTEES

Where the truster has given discretion to the trustees, the court will not seek to control the way in which the trustees exercise this discretion unless they are committing a breach of trust or acting in a clearly unreasonable way. The trustees cannot ask the court to "rubber stamp" their exercise of discretion. On the other hand, the trustees are not entitled to stand back and refuse to exercise a discretionary power or, as Lord President Dunedin put it, they cannot simply "button their pockets and say that they will not exercise any discretion whatever": *Train* v *Buchanan's Trs* (1907).

While the discretion of trustees will not be fettered by the court, it must be exercised in a reasonable manner. This means that they must take account of the circumstances in which discretion is being exercised and exercise their discretion in good faith, carefully, impartially and in the spirit of seeking to perform their duty as trustees to the best of their ability: *Board of Management for Dundee General Hospitals* v *Bell's Trs* (1952). If a trustee has a personal interest in the outcome of an exercise of discretion, he ought to decline to participate in that exercise.

Trustees are entitled to take legal advice on how best to exercise their discretion and they may discuss the pros and cons, if they choose, with the beneficiaries. The court will not intervene unless there is a clear allegation of bad faith on the part of the trustees. The case of *Martin* v *Edinburgh District Council* (1988) is an example of a case where the trustees failed to take professional advice and did not apply their minds, when making a discretionary decision in respect of investment policy, to the best interests of the beneficiaries. In that case, the court reviewed the grounds on which discretion was exercised and found that the council had been in breach of trust. They failed to exercise their discretion in a reasonable way consistent with their fiduciary duty to the beneficiaries.

The unreasonable exercise of discretion may relate to the way in which trustees decide to dispose of trust assets. If given discretion to grant relief to a class of persons, the trustees may act unreasonably if they decide, as they did in *Thomson* v *Davidson's Trs* (1888), to pay a clearly inadequate sum when more could be afforded. However, the court will not lightly interfere with trustees acting reasonably in the discharge of their discretionary power. Where the truster specifies that a discretionary decision made by his trustees is to be final or that their discretion is absolute, the court has no place to intervene at all.

DEADLOCK

In the event of disagreement among trustees, the only remedy is to petition the *nobile officium* of the Court of Session in order to ask the court to appoint a new trustee in order to resolve any deadlock. No statutory provision permits the resolution of deadlock.

DELEGATION

Unless the trust deed states otherwise, trustees have the power under s 4(1)(f) of the Trusts (Scotland) Act 1921 to appoint factors and agents and pay them suitable remuneration. At common law, trustees have a wider power to appoint and pay agents or managers provided that a reasonably prudent person would appoint such an agent in relation to their own affairs. For tasks they are not qualified to perform, trustees have a duty to appoint an agent (see Chapter 6). However, this power cannot be exercised to employ someone to do what the trustees themselves ought to do.

There is, therefore, an important distinction in regard to the kind of task that may be delegated. Trustees cannot allow an agent to exercise the discretion which they, as trustees, are bound to exercise. However, they can delegate to an agent administrative functions. In other words, the truster has placed faith in the judgement of the trustees and the existing trustees have placed faith in the judgement of any trustees they assume. Therefore the trustees alone should exercise the discretionary power they have to determine how trust purposes should be carried out and how trust income should be distributed. The trust itself, the exercise of the office of trustee, cannot be delegated; however, the fulfilment of some of the administrative tasks of the office may be delegated to a suitably qualified agent.

Although this distinction is clear in principle, the Scottish Law Commission has pointed out that in practice it may be a difficult one to draw (Discussion Paper on *The Nature and Constitution of Trusts* (Scot Law Com No 133, 2006), para 3.9). In a large trust, the assets of which may include a business, it may be necessary to appoint a manager of that business who would require significant discretion in order to oversee its operation. It would be impractical to refer to trustees to take every decision which may have financial implications for the trust estate. Likewise, a fund manager requires an independent sphere of discretion in managing the funds of others and any reasonable person, when dealing with their own shares, would grant that discretion provided that the manager was working within pre-determined boundaries. Otherwise, opportunities for profit, or for minimising loss, might be missed. Investment decisions, therefore, may be delegated but not decisions about the application of income from the investments: *Scott* v *Occidental Petroleum (Caledonia) Ltd* (1990).

Trustees, even when they have exercised due care in selecting an agent, may be liable for breach of trust if they convey title to trust property to that agent. Placing trust assets beyond their control would render the trustees in breach of their duty to secure trust property. The transfer of title to a third party or an agent incurs risk for the trustees who, as unsecured creditors, would have only a personal right to recover the value of the property in the event of the sequestration of the third party. For any sum they could not recover, they would be personally liable to the trust estate: *Mustard* v *Mortimer's Trs* (1899). The transfer of trust money to an agent may be necessary for the carrying out of trust business. If so, the trustees will be safe from liability if they ensure that they do not transfer an excessive sum and that the trust money is kept separate from the agent's personal funds: *Ferguson* v *Paterson* (1898).

The Scottish Law Commission favours the introduction of a law whereby trustees may be authorised by statute, unless prohibited by the trust deed, to convey trust property to nominees (Scot Law Com No 133, para 3.28). However, such an authorisation would be circumscribed by the duty of trustees to select an appropriate nominee and take appropriate steps to minimise the potential risks involved.

CO-TRUSTEES AS JOINT PROPRIETORS

Joint property is not the same as common property and much of the logic of trust administration flows from the simple fact that trustees own trust property jointly and not in common. Common owners can each identify a separable *pro indiviso* share in their common property. They might, for instance, own a third each. Trustees cannot do that with trust property. It is owned by the trustees for the time being and the trustees act together as a body. They have no separable share in the trust property and can only administer it on a joint basis. They do so at the risk of joint and several liability. This links back to the idea of dual patrimonies. If T, acting as a trustee, incurs a debt through an act of trust administration, for example under a contract with a third party, then he and his co-trustees are jointly and severally liable under that contract up to the value of the estate which they hold in trust (ie the trust patrimony). They are not personally liable. If T and his fellow trustees are in breach of trust, for example through negligently incurring a debt while acting as trustees, they attract personal liability for their negligence. They were entitled to enter a contract as trustees administering the trust; they were not entitled to act negligently and in breach of trust. Their personal liability is, again, joint and several. However, in this case it affects their personal patrimony, not the trust patrimony.

LIABILITY FOR DECISIONS

Trustees may be liable to beneficiaries, to the truster or to third parties. There are many potential bases for liability, such as failure to account, negligence or acting *ultra vires* (that is, trustees acting beyond their powers). The remedies available to co-trustees, beneficiaries and the truster in respect of maladministration of the trust are set out on pages 101–110.

Essential Facts

- All trustees must have a reasonable opportunity to participate in decisions affecting the administration of the trust.
- Trustees who have a personal interest in a decision will not count as part of the quorum.
- In modern law, a physical meeting of trustees is probably unnecessary, but all trustees have the right to be consulted and the usual rule is that decisions are valid if taken by a quorum of trustees. A quorum is the majority of all the accepting and surviving trustees qualified to vote, not simply the majority of those present at a meeting.
- The court will generally not interfere with the exercise of discretion by trustees.
- Trustees may employ agents and may delegate some of their functions, but they cannot delegate the office of trustee or the discretion which they themselves must exercise as trustees.
- As joint owners of trust property, trustees must act together as a body.

Essential Cases

Wyse v Abbott (1881): two out of the three trustees in a trust executed a deed of assumption, assuming two additional trustees. They did so without consulting Mr Wyse, the third trustee, who only found out some months later. The court held that the nomination of the additional trustees was invalid and their assumption was void. It was of the essence of the duty of a body of trustees that they should meet and exchange views on the trust affairs. The trustees had denied Mr Wyse the opportunity to express his view.

Malcolm v Goldie (1895): one of five surviving trustees in a trust went to live permanently in Australia. The remaining trustees assumed two new trustees on the basis that the trustee who had emigrated had ceased to act. The court held that the assumption, approved by a quorum of trustees, was valid even though no notice of it was given to the trustee who lived abroad. The requirement to consult a trustee did not impose an absolute requirement to obtain his opinion. The trustees need only afford him an opportunity to appear. Since this trustee resided in Australia with no intention of returning, there was no point in even giving him notice. Had he been accessible, they were bound to give him notice of their meeting so that he might give his view on the appointment. In normal circumstances, it would have been wrong to exclude him from deliberations. (Note that, over a century on, notions of accessibility have now developed and this decision is unlikely to be followed today.)

Scott v Occidental Petroleum (Caledonia) Ltd (1990): in a settlement, a widow received damages arising from the Piper Alpha disaster for herself and as tutrix (ie the guardian of a pupil child in the law as it was at that time) for her children. The court was asked to approve draft trust deeds whereby the widow would act as one of the trustees and administer trust funds for the benefit of each of her children. The court refused to approve the arrangement. It was held that a tutrix could appoint a factor or agent to perform acts of administration, particularly where the business of the trust required continual attention. The arrangement in this case, however, went too far since it amounted to the delegation to trustees of all the powers and duties of the tutrix herself, including the power of daily management and of decision-making in respect of the trust funds. If the tutrix had resigned (and she had the power to do so under the 1921 Act), then her role in the administration of the trust would have disappeared altogether. It is not possible for a trustee to delegate his trust and, while an agent may be appointed, the trustee cannot surrender his own judgement to the discretion of others. This arrangement would have permitted such a surrender and therefore the court could not approve of it.

6 DUTIES OF TRUSTEES

The primary duty of trustees is to carry out the trust purposes with due care. In doing so, they are bound to exercise their powers "in good faith in the presumed interest" of the beneficiaries and not to advance their own personal preferences: *Train v Buchanan's Trs* (1907). In exercising their powers in administering the trust, the trustees come under a number of general and specific duties. The duty not to act as *auctor in rem suam* is discussed separately in Chapter 7.

THE GENERAL DUTY OF CARE

A trustee must bring to the administration of the trust the same care and diligence which a person of ordinary prudence may be expected to use in the management of his own affairs: *Raes v Meek* (1889). His conduct, therefore, will be measured against an external, objective, standard. What counts is not what the trustee would have done when managing his own affairs but what a person of ordinary prudence would have done in the same circumstances when dealing with his property.

There is an absence of authority on the point, but this test seems to apply regardless of whether the trustee is a lay person or one who is professionally qualified and acting in the course of his business or profession. In English law, a higher standard of care is to be expected from a professional trustee than from one who is acting gratuitously. Section 1(1) of the Trustee Act 2000, which applies only in England and Wales, requires a professional trustee to exercise reasonable care and skill and, in particular, to exercise such special knowledge or experience as it would be reasonable to expect of a person acting in the course of that kind of business or profession. The Scottish Law Commission has suggested a similar statutory rule for Scotland where someone acts as a trustee in the course of his business or profession (Discussion Paper on *Breach of Trust* (Scot Law Com No 123, 2003), para 3.4). At the same time, the Commission has proposed replacing the common law duty with a statutory one requiring a minimum standard from all trustees. This would be that the trustee must use the same care and diligence that a person of ordinary prudence would use in managing the affairs of others. This follows the view that even prudent people are generally more careful in relation to the affairs of others than they are in relation to their own affairs.

SPECIFIC DUTIES

The duty to conserve and protect the trust estate

In line with the general duty of care, a trustee must do what a person of ordinary prudence would be expected to do in maintaining the value of the trust estate. If the estate contains heritable property, then it must be properly maintained and kept in good repair. This duty may extend to making alterations or to refurbishment if the property is let out. However, risky or unnecessarily expensive alterations, or work that is not in the best interests of the trust estate, should be avoided. The court cannot be asked by trustees to approve capital expenditure in advance: it is a matter for their discretion and subject to their duty to act as persons of ordinary prudence would do. Conservation of the estate will include the duty to insure it against normal risks. In general, trustees should not act wastefully or extravagantly with the trust estate; for example, they should not engage in litigation without good cause for doing so.

The duty to secure trust property

Trustees are under a duty to take possession of the trust estate. This means taking title to trust property and maintaining that property within their control. Leaving trust property in the hands of a third party will result in personal liability for the trustees if that property is lost (for example by the third party being sequestrated). Trust funds in the bank should be in a separate account for the benefit of the trust and this account should not be allowed to be under the sole control of one trustee (unless he is the only trustee) or the trust solicitor.

The duty to distribute the estate to the correct person

Trustees are under a duty to make payments from the trust estate to the correct person, be it a beneficiary or a creditor. If they fail to do so, even if they are in good faith, they are liable to compensate the correct person for the full amount with interest from the date the payment was due. The trustees have it in their power to establish who the correct payee is, and to require them to prove their entitlement, before making payment. Since the trustees, if they are unsure, can protect themselves by seeking judicial authority, and the warrant of the court, for making the payment, the law imposes a particularly stringent duty upon them to pay the correct person. If there is doubt, payment should be withheld until the doubt is resolved: for example *Corbridge* v *Fraser* (1915). Recovery against a payee who was not entitled to receive a distribution might be made, under the general principles of unjustified enrichment, using the *condictio indebiti*. In the meantime, the trustees remain liable to the correct payee to account for what ought to have been paid and, in addition, for interest thereon from the date when payment should have been made.

If a payment is made in error, trustees may escape liability in several circumstances, including the following three. First, if the correct payee somehow misled them into making, in good faith, a payment to the wrong person, then the correct payee would be personally barred from raising an objection. Second, in the context of an executry, the executors may, once 6 months have elapsed from the date of death, distribute the estate provided that they reasonably believe that the estate is solvent and that there are no unidentified outstanding claims due by the estate. If a beneficiary cannot be traced, it is possible to take out missing beneficiaryinsurance to protect against liability should he subsequently appear. Third, under s 32 of the Trusts (Scotland) Act 1921, the court may relieve trustees of personal liability for any breach of trust if they have acted honestly and reasonably and ought fairly to be excused. Given the heavy onus on them to take care in distributing the trust estate, they may find limited solace in s 32, although its operation cannot be ruled out. For example, if the trustees, on the basis of erroneous legal advice, misconstrue the trust deed and, in good faith, make an incorrect payment, then it may apply: *Re Allsop* (1914).

The Scottish Law Commission has raised the possibility of trustees being made subject to a statutory duty obliging them to inform any person that they are a beneficiary in the trust (Discussion Paper on *Supplementary Miscellaneous Issues relating to Trust Law* (Scot Law Com No 148, 2011), para 10.5). The common law seems to impose no such requirement. The whole area of disclosure by trustees is likely to be subject to new legislation.

The duty to pay at the right time

The trustees must distribute trust property at the time directed by the truster, unless a delay is caused by circumstances beyond his control. If there is a delay due to the fault of the trustees, then the trustees will be personally liable for interest. If trust property, during the delay, depreciates in value, then the trustees will be liable for that depreciation if the delay was their fault. However, if the title of the beneficiary is disputed and an action is raised then the trustees may legitimately delay payment until the dispute is resolved.

The duty to keep trust accounts

Trustees have a duty to maintain proper accounts recording their intromissions with the trust estate. This is usually implied in every trust, although it can be excluded expressly or by implication: *Leitch* v *Leitch* (1927). These should show how much was spent, to whom it was paid and why, and vouchers and receipts should be retained. A beneficiary, even if his interest is contingent, is entitled to inspect the accounts and the vouchers and may obtain a copy at his own expense: per Lord Avonside in *Murray* v *Cameron* (1969). There is no entitlement to receive a copy of the accounts at the trust's expense, except in the case of a residuary legatee. Keeping proper accounts is a protection for the trustee who is only entitled to deduct such expenditure as he can prove was necessarily made in connection with trust administration.

The duty to oversee co-trustees

A trustee has a duty to oversee the actions of his co-trustees. Section 3(d) of the Trusts (Scotland) Act 1921, regarded as being declaratory of the common law, places in all trusts, unless the trust deed excludes it, a provision that each trustee shall be liable only for his own acts and intromissions and shall not be liable for the acts and intromissions of co-trustees and shall not be liable for omissions. This means that a trustee will only be liable for what he himself does, or fails to do, and not for what his predecessors may have done or failed to do: *Mackenzie's Exr* v *Thomson's Trs* (1965).

What this section, or the common law, does not do, however, is to exempt a trustee from liability for the breaches of trust of his co-trustees where he himself is in breach of trust. Trustees are supposed to act together in the administration of the trust and no trustee should neglect to involve himself. As Lord President Robertson put it, a trustee "is not entitled to purchase a quiet life at the expense of the estate": *Millar's Trs* v *Polson* (1897). If a trustee negligently prevents his co-trustees from committing a breach of trust, that will be, in itself, a breach of trust. The same is true if the trustee authorises a breach by his fellow trustees. No trustee is entitled to disclaim responsibility where he ought to have known that his fellow trustees were acting in breach of trust and he allowed them to proceed.

The Scottish Law Commission regards s 3(d) as misleading and proposes its amendment in order to find a balance between demanding too high a standard of vigilance, on the one hand, and preventing "sleeping trustees" from avoiding liability on the other (Scot Law Com No 123 (2003), paras 7.5–7.7). It proposes making a trustee liable for his own acts or omissions, or the failure to take reasonable steps to ensure that a co-trustee does not commit a breach of trust.

Trustees are liable on a joint and several basis for the loss caused to the trust estate. Therefore any one or more of them can be sued for the entire loss, with a right of relief against the remainder for their respective shares of liability. The proportion of fault of each trustee is irrelevant: they all share equally in liability for any loss.

The duty not to avoid trust administration

A trustee voluntarily accepts the responsibility of engaging in the administration of the trust. That does not impose an absolute duty to attend every trust meeting or to be involved in every trust decision, since that would be unworkable in practice. Even a trustee *sine qua non* might not be able to attend every meeting, although in his case no valid decision could be taken without him. However, accepting responsibility as a trustee imposes a duty not to turn a blind eye to trust administration or to refuse to become involved.

The duty to appoint agents in certain circumstances

Trustees, when faced in the administration of the trust with tasks beyond their own expertise or skill, fall under a common law duty to employ suitable agents. This duty arises in circumstances where an agent would be appointed by a reasonably prudent person when looking after the affairs of others. In selecting agents, trustees should appoint only those whom they reasonably believe to be competent and reputable. They have a duty to exercise reasonable supervision of any agent they appoint.

INVESTMENT DUTIES

The power of investment

A trust deed may restrict the options of trustees when it comes to investment and may require them to invest in particular areas or to avoid particular investments or types of investment. Trustees must obviously adhere to this. However, where the trust deed is silent, s 4(1)(ea) of the Trusts (Scotland) Act 1921 gives trustees the power to make "any kind of investment". This does not mean that trustees have carte blanche to make any investment. It simply means they can invest in any type of property, be it heritable, moveable or incorporeal (for example, shares). Any investment will now be an authorised investment under the 1921 Act, therefore, unless the truster has specifically narrowed the trustees' power of investment. However, even if they have the power to invest, not every investment will be one which trustees should properly make.

Duties imposed on trustees in regard to investment

The duties of trustees when exercising the power of investment are governed largely by ss 4A–4C of the Trusts (Scotland) Act (this was the result of amendment by the Charities and Trustee Investment (Scotland) Act 2005) although some common law principles continue to apply.

Although trustees are absolute owners of trust property, they do not have the usual range of discretion of absolute owners when it comes to making investment decisions. This is because the law seeks to protect the interests of the beneficiaries by imposing general duties on trustees. In this context, these general duties principally require that trustees should, when making investment decisions, act in the best interests of the trust and avoid any conflict between those interests and their personal interests.

The duty to obtain and consider advice

Before investing, a trustee should obtain and consider proper advice about the way in which the power to invest should be exercised (s 4A(2)). "Proper advice" means advice from someone reasonably believed by the trustee to be qualified by their ability and practical experience of financial and other matters relating to the proposed investment (s 4A(5)). This depends on the context. If investment in shares was intended, advice from a stockbroker or some similar financial adviser would be appropriate; if the investment were in art or classic cars, then it would be proper to obtain advice from an expert adviser in the relevant field. While, as a matter of trust law, the advice need not be given in writing, it would be prudent for trustees to ensure that it was. The duty to take advice is more stringent than the general duty of care currently imposed on trustees. A person of ordinary prudence, in managing his own affairs, may be happy to make a particular investment, whereas if acting as a trustee that person may be under a duty in the first instance to take proper advice.

The duty to obtain advice is not absolute and no advice need be sought where a trustee reasonably concludes that in all the circumstances it is unnecessary or inappropriate to obtain it (s 4A(4)). Note from this that the decision not to seek advice from a qualified and experienced third party must be reasonable (ie it is subject to an external standard of conduct). Seeking advice may reasonably be inappropriate, for example when the trust fund is small and the cost of obtaining proper independent advice disproportionate when the trustees intend to place the fund in an interest-bearing account. Independent advice from a third party may reasonably be unnecessary where, for instance, the trustee, or one of the trustees, can demonstrate that he has personal expertise in investment matters.

When advice is obtained, it must be considered. However, trustees should not blindly follow it, since the power to make investment decisions belongs to the trustees and should not be delegated. On the other hand, unless the trust deed excludes it, trustees do have the power to delegate invest-ment management functions (s 4C) and may appoint an agent to manage investments (for example, to buy and sell shares and identify investment opportunities). Again, if this is not excluded by the trust purposes, trustees may, in order to exercise their power of investment, appoint a nominee to carry out acts in regard to as much of the trust estate as they may determine (s 4B). Such an appointment must be made in writing and the nominee must, in the reasonable belief of the trustees, have the necessary skills, knowledge and expertise to deal with trust property.

Specific duties in regard to investment

When making an investment decision, under s 4A(1), trustees must have regard to:

(a) the suitability to the trust of the proposed investment; and
(b) the need for diversification of investments of the trust, in so far as is appropriate to the circumstances of the trust.

Suitability to the trust of the proposed investment should be construed in terms of the purposes of the trust. Simply because the truster was known to be a vehement anti-smoker, for example, would not preclude the trustees from investing in a tobacco company, provided that the trust deed did not exclude the power to do so and such investment was in line with trust purposes. But if the trust purpose was to invest to generate income to benefit those suffering ill effects from consuming tobacco products, then any investment by the trustees in such products would appear to be unsuitable in terms of s 4A. In making decisions about investment, trustees must be properly motivated and must act in the interests of the trust and its beneficiaries and not for motives of their own (see "Proper motivation" below).

Diversification is about protecting trust property against undue risk. When Antonio said in *The Merchant of Venice* (Act 1, Scene 1) "My ventures are not in one bottom trusted, Nor to one place", he meant that his merchandise was not all placed in a single trading vessel, implying that he had spread the risk of loss at sea by placing his goods in more than one vessel. This is what diversification means: spreading the risk of investments so as to avoid placing too high a proportion of a fund in any one company or economic sector or, even, in any single geographical region. In this way, the whole fund is not exposed to the failure of one sector. What constitutes appropriate diversification is a matter of degree and will depend on the size of the trust fund to be invested. It would not be appropriate for trustees to be under a duty to diversify a small trust fund where the expense or inconvenience of doing so was unreasonable (particularly where professional advice would have to be taken), or the potential benefit to the trust would be negligible.

The duty to review investments

Once an investment is made, trustees remain under a common law duty to review that investment periodically. Section 4A(3) refers to the need, when reviewing investments, to consider proper advice about whether the investments should be varied. There are two duties here. First, what constitutes a proper periodic review of investments will depend on the nature of the investment. Where the investment is in a particularly volatile area of the market, this may require a very regular review of the value of investments whereas in other circumstances a quarterly or bi-annual or even an annual review may suffice. Second, the need to review investments makes it clear that trustees cannot simply retain shares or place funds in a current or deposit account and leave them there indefinitely: *Clarke* v *Clarke's Trs* (1925). Deciding not to invest in a fund is in itself an investment decision. The requirement to take proper advice helps to ensure that trustees do not take inappropriate risks with trust property. Risk, in itself, is not a virtue and trustees should not take great risks with trust funds unless the trust purposes give them clear instructions to do so. At the same time, they should attempt to protect the value of the fund in real terms and low-risk, ultra-safe, investments, or hiding the fund under their bed, would not achieve that end. In part this is because the value of the fund in real terms may be reduced due to inflation, but to act in this way would be in breach of the trustees' duty to exercise judgement in relation to investment: *Melville* v *Noble's Trs* (1896).

Proper motivation

Trustees should not bring into the management of the trust estate their own religious, political, cultural or moral views, if these are not relevant to the carrying out of the trust purposes: *Martin* v *Edinburgh District Council* (1988). It is part of his fiduciary duty that a trustee, in any act of trust administration, must take into account both the trust purposes and the interests of the beneficiaries. Any trustee who is unduly influenced by other considerations risks placing his private beliefs in conflict with the trust purposes. That may lead to invalid decisions being taken for misdirected reasons.

Likewise, the trustee is not entitled to guess what a deceased truster, in the light of his own known preferences or circumstances, might have decided to do. Such speculative considerations are not relevant: it is the wording of the trust purposes that counts. Of course, a trustee will have private beliefs that are impossible to divorce from decisions that he makes in trust administration, but the decision must be consistent with trust purposes and must be taken in the interests of the beneficiaries and not simply to satisfy the personal motive of the trustee. On the other hand, it is open to a truster expressly to authorise a trustee to apply his personal values when deciding which transactions to enter, or when entering transactions of a particular type. Alternatively, if all the beneficiaries, being fully informed, consent once such a transaction has been completed, then the trustee's decision will be valid.

REMEDIES

A beneficiary has a range of remedies in the event that a trustee is in breach of trust. These remedies are not mutually exclusive; for instance, an interdict to prevent the continuation of a breach of trust may be brought together with an action for damages in respect of losses caused to the estate up to the cessation of the offending behaviour. Nor are the following remedies necessarily limited to beneficiaries.

Interdict

A beneficiary, co-trustee or truster may seek an interdict to prevent the trustees from undertaking an intended act, or to stop them from continuing with an act, which is in breach of trust. Once a breach is complete, and no repetition is apprehended, then interdict is not a competent remedy.

Damages

A trustee is bound to make good loss to the trust estate caused by his breach of trust. The absence of causation is therefore a defence for the trustee. If he can establish that the loss would have occurred even if he had not been in breach of duty, he will not be liable.

The amount of damages is equal to the loss suffered by the trust. The loss need not be foreseeable or reasonable and the degree of fault is not relevant to the measure of damages. The liability to make good the loss will arise, therefore, regardless of whether the loss results from deliberate embezzlement or mere error of judgement.

A breach of trust may lead to a profit, rather than a loss. Where this happens, it is sometimes said that the trustee holds the profit as a constructive trustee. But this seems illogical, for the trustee is already a trustee. An alternative view is that the profit, having been generated with part of the trust patrimony, becomes part of that patrimony and at no stage enters the personal patrimony of the trustee. The profit is part of the trust and no new "constructive" trust is necessary. The trustee therefore remains personally liable to account to the trustee for the profit.

It is a rule in the law of trusts that where a trustee enters into more than one transaction, and some transactions produce a loss while others produce a gain, it is not possible to set a loss off against a gain. The trustee is personally liable to make good the loss but the gain, which belongs to the trust patrimony, is not available to him to use for that purpose. However, only the loss on a completed transaction is said to count. Where losses and gains are made which form part of a single complete transaction, then the trustee can have that transaction taken as a whole and will have no liability if the profit cancels out the loss (A Mackenzie Stuart, *The Law of Trusts* (1932), p 375). This latter idea is a difficult one, since it may not be clear what constitutes a complete transaction. The relevant question appears to be whether two transactions made in breach of trust, loss-making transaction A, which was distinct from profit-making transaction B, were part and parcel of the same transaction. If they were, the profit may be balanced against the loss to determine the overall measure of profit or loss. There is no case law on this issue in Scotland.

Accounting

A beneficiary is entitled to raise an action of count, reckoning and payment to force a trustee to account to him for this share of the trust estate. Unlike an action of damages, the obligation to account is not subject to a 5-year prescriptive period. In fact, it is imprescriptible: Prescription and Limitation (Scotland) Act 1973, Sch 3, para e(i). However, any underlying liability to make payment for losses does prescribe after 20 years.

Removal of trustees

A petition for the removal of a trustee may be brought by any beneficiary or a co-trustee. The power of the court, at common law and under statute, to remove a trustee is discussed in Chapter 4.

AVOIDING LIABILITY

Section 31 of the Trusts (Scotland) Act 1921

This provides that where a trustee commits a breach of trust at the instigation or request of a beneficiary, or with his written consent, then the court has discretion to apply all or some of that beneficiary's interest in the trust in order to indemnify the trustee. This advances the common law, which merely personally bars any trustee from raising an action against a trustee for any breach to which he had consented in advance. If this defence is established, it means that the trustee may be authorised not to pay the beneficiary his full interest in the trust; he is therefore able to use that interest to satisfy the claims of other beneficiaries. It does not mean that the trustee can raise his own action against the indemnifying beneficiary. Note that, unlike consent, any instigation or request need not be written, but it must still be proved on a balance of probabilities.

Section 32 of the Trusts (Scotland) Act 1921

This provision gives the court power to relieve a trustee of personal liability for breach of trust where the trustee "has acted honestly and reasonably, and ought fairly to be excused". It may do so in full or in part. A dishonest trustee is unlikely to be relieved of liability. Whether conduct is reasonable may depend on whether it was in good faith and whether it was based on an excusable error. For example, trustees might be relieved of liability for an honest but mistaken interpretation of an ambiguous provision in a trust deed which they made in good faith. It may also depend on whether the trustee was acting gratuitously; the court may be less forgiving of a trustee who is remunerated. Any relief granted, of course, will prejudice those who may have a claim against the trustee and this is likely to be taken into account when deciding whether it is fair to grant it.

Immunity clauses

Apart from the general law, a truster may attempt to restrict or entirely remove liability for his trustees by using an immunity clause. It is clear that such a clause cannot protect trustees from personal liability for the consequences of acts of administration undertaken in bad faith (ie fraud) or with gross negligence (*culpa lata*). The concept of gross negligence, and what differentiates it from ordinary negligence, is not much discussed in the case law, although the Scottish Law Commission is of the view that nonetheless it is "a workable concept" (Scot Law Com No 123 (2003), para 3.30), despite the lack of a clear definitional borderline between gross negligence and ordinary negligence. Gross negligence, or gross breach of duty, is based on fault that goes beyond mere carelessness. It suggests an indifference to the consequences for the beneficiaries of an act of trustee administration or the disregarding of an obvious risk; in short, so serious a departure from the standard expected of a trustee that it cannot be excused.

Where a trustee acting in good faith is simply negligent, and this causes loss to the trust estate, any clause purporting to exempt him from personal liability will still be interpreted narrowly by the court. A trustee may nonetheless be protected by a suitably drafted immunity clause where he commits a mere error of judgement, provided that he does so while attempting, in good faith, to benefit the trust and its beneficiaries, and so long as he was not acting in violation of one of his plain duties as a trustee: *Knox* v *Mackinnon* (1886).

Proposals for reform

The Scottish Law Commission, in its discussion paper, has suggested that the law in this area needs to be clarified. There are pros and cons to the use of immunity clauses. They allow risks to be allocated clearly in advance and, if they did not exist, people might decline to accept office as a trustee. On the other hand, such clauses may unfairly protect the trustees at the expense of the beneficiaries and they might encourage risk-taking by trustees.

The Commission is of the view that professional trustees (those acting as trustees in the course of their business or profession) should always be liable for any breach of their duty of care, regardless of any immunity clause. It is fairer that such losses are borne by the trustee in this case (who may insure against it, or carry professional indemnity insurance as standard) rather than the beneficiaries. Where lay trustees are concerned, the Commission favours retaining the current rule where there is liability for gross negligence but not for ordinary negligence. In a trust containing both types of trustees, where all were negligent but the lay trustees were immune, the professional trustees could not seek relief from them on the basis of joint and several liability. The lay trustees would be shielded by the immunity clause: if they are not liable, they cannot be jointly and severally liable either (the latter concept demands that all parties are liable, at least to some extent). It is also proposed that any attempt to lower the standard of care expected of a trustee by means of a term in the trust deed should be ineffective (Scot Law Com No 123 (2003), para 3.52).

Essential Facts

- A trustee is under a general duty of care to exercise the same care and diligence as a person of ordinary prudence is expected to use in the management of his own affairs.
- Trustees are under a number of specific duties in respect of their administrative role – they must pay the correct person; secure trust property; maintain accounts; and oversee the activities of their fellow trustees.
- A range of duties exist in respect of the exercise of the power of investment: trustees must usually obtain and consider professional advice before investing; they must diversify investments and ought

to review them periodically; they must make investment decisions based on the interests of the trust and its beneficiaries; and must not give vent to their own personal preferences.

- There is limited indemnity for trustees under statute where a breach of trust has been instigated, requested or consented to in writing by a beneficiary.
- There is further potential protection under statute where a trustee has incurred personal liability for breach of trust but has acted honestly and reasonably and ought fairly to be excused.
- An immunity clause will not protect a trustee from liability for gross negligence or fraud, but may do so for ordinary negligence.

Essential Cases

Lutea Trustees Ltd v Orbis Trustees Guernsey Ltd (1997): professional trustees, at the request of the truster, loaned a large sum to an individual to be repaid soon after, taking as security shares which proved to be worthless. The loan was not repaid. The trustees then resigned and were given a deed of indemnification by the new assumed trustees. The assumed trustees then brought an action for damages for breach of trust. The court held that the trustees were guilty of gross negligence (*culpa lata*) in making the loan on the terms they did and that it was open to the court to conclude this even in the absence of any averment of gross negligence by the pursuer. The trustees had no right to indemnity in respect of their gross negligence. Opinion was reserved as to whether the standard of care for professional trustees was higher than that required of gratuitous trustees.

Tibbert v McColl (1994): the trustees of a private pension fund paid a cheque, intended to cover the pursuer's pension, into their own company's current account (which was then overdrawn). No separate trust account existed. The pursuer, who had taken early retirement, disputed the sum to be paid and it remained in the account when the company later went into liquidation. The court held that the trustees were in breach of trust for paying the cheque into a company account that was at the risk of the company's creditors. Since the account was overdrawn, the funds were thereby alienated and placed out of the trustees' control. A man of ordinary prudence in the management of his own affairs would not place trust funds into a bank account in the name of a third party; nor would he place trust funds into a third party's bank account which was overdrawn, particularly at a time when, as here, the third party was engaged in litigation with others.

Martin v Edinburgh District Council (1988): the council, which managed 58 trust funds, adopted a policy, in opposition to apartheid, of disinvesting from those trust funds in South Africa. The policy was developed without any consideration of trust law. An action was raised for declarator that the council was in breach of fiduciary duties incumbent upon it by directing stockbrokers to prepare an alternative scheme of investment which they then put into effect by divesting themselves of South African investments in pursuit of their policy. The court held that the council failed in "a prime duty" as trustees by failing to apply their minds to the question of whether this change in investment policy was in the best interests of the beneficiaries; they also failed in their duty by neglecting to obtain professional advice as to whether what they proposed was in the beneficiaries' interests.

Knox v Mackinnon (1886): the truster set up a trust in which his widow was to receive an annuity for life and the residue was divided among his children. The trustees had the fullest powers of investment and advanced substantial sums to one of the children, without informing the others. These advances were made on insufficient security, causing loss to the trust estate. A clause in the trust deed declared that trustees "shall not be liable for omissions, errors, or neglect of management … but each shall be liable for his own actual intromissions only". The court held that this clause afforded no protection for the consequences of *culpa lata* or gross negligence by the trustees. It may afford protection to trustees who have in good faith abstained from closely superintending trust administration, or who have committed mere errors of judgement while acting to benefit the trust and the beneficiaries. However, the trustees here had been guilty of gross neglect of duty, having failed to exercise the degree of care and prudence expected of them and having entered into a transaction into which no man of ordinary prudence would have entered. It was stated, *obiter*, that the fact that they knowingly relied on advice from the borrower's law agent did not assist the

trustees; no-one in their fiduciary position should imperil the beneficiaries by relying on partial advice.

Nouillan v Nouillan's Trs (1991): in an action of accounting, the
pursuers (the beneficiaries of a trust) argued that they required to see
the source materials upon which statements of account were based
in order to reconcile them with the trust accounts. The court held
that the beneficiaries were entitled to see the vouchers for the intromissions of the trustees. Lord Clyde stated that trustees were bound
to give a beneficiary full information about their administration and
to let him see the vouchers (ie receipts for expenditure) as well as
the accounts.

Melville v Noble's Trs (1896): trustees left a substantial trust fund
on deposit receipt with a bank for 19 years. During this time they
did not consider the question of investment. The court held that
this was a breach of trust on the basis of a total neglect of the duty
of care. A man of ordinary prudence would not have dealt with his
own funds in this way; he would have sought to invest it so that it
would yield a higher return and that is what the trustees should have
done. Investment of this type may be a good temporary expedient
but it was not a permanent investment. However, the trustees had
not applied their minds to the question of investment of the trust
funds and they had a duty to do so.

7 CONFLICT OF INTEREST

Trustees are in a fiduciary relationship both to the truster (since they are bound to carry out his purposes in good faith) and to the beneficiaries who have an interest in the proper administration of the trust. Alongside the division between a trustee's personal property and the property which they hold in trust for beneficiaries (the idea of separate patrimonies), there is a requirement that trustees clearly separate their personal interests from the interests of the trust. They must avoid placing themselves in a position where these two interests may conflict. This is a particular feature of trust law because trustees own the trust property and the beneficiaries merely have a personal right to have it conveyed to them when certain conditions are met. This puts trustees in a strong position and makes it relatively easy for them to commit fraud. Therefore, to prevent the possibility of conflicts arising, the law rigidly precludes a trustee from being *auctor in rem suam*.

AUCTOR IN REM SUAM

A trustee must not be *auctor in rem suam* (literally, one who causes increase in his own thing). This means that the trustee must avoid creating a situation where there is a conflict between his personal interests and the interests of the trust. His decisions as trustee should be in the interests of the beneficiaries and should never be taken in order to advance his own interests. There are several reasons why this principle has been adopted. First, a conflict may prevent a trustee from fulfilling his duties to the trust. The most obvious example would arise where the trustee wanted to purchase trust property: it would be in his personal interests to buy at the lowest possible price but as a trustee it would be his duty to sell at the highest price he could. Such a conflict would be irreconcilable; therefore the law, as a general rule, prevents it from arising. Second, the principle protects the trustee's ability to act in a fiduciary capacity; without it, his ability to transact in good faith may be compromised. Third, trustees have knowledge of trust affairs which third parties dealing at arm's length would not have and it is regarded as unfair to allow them to use such knowledge to their own benefit: *Hamilton* v *Wright* (1842).

The rule against a trustee being *auctor in rem suam* is applied strictly. It is irrelevant whether a transaction is perfectly fair, or the trust estate would gain a benefit and suffer no loss as a result of it. The trustee will be in breach of trust and the transaction will be voidable. This is so even if the trustee entered the transaction in good faith. Any profit which the trustee may have made must be paid back to the trust estate, even if the estate itself suffered no loss. It is sometimes said that a constructive trust is created over any profit which a trustee makes in these circumstances. This means that it is irrebuttably presumed that the trustee holds any such profit on behalf of the trust and that it does not enter his personal patrimony. But this has been doubted because the law on constructive trust in Scotland appears to rest upon very weak foundations.

A transaction entered into in breach of the principle *auctor in rem suam* may be challenged by any beneficiary who has title and interest to do so; by any co-trustee or by the truster, at least if he has a reversionary right in the trust estate. If the truster does have a reversionary right, his creditors may also challenge the transaction, as can a judicial factor appointed to the trust estate. The right to challenge the transaction and have it rendered void will be lost if the challenger had consented to, or acquiesced in, the breach of trust.

Exceptions

There is an important exception to the application of the principle. A trustee may act as *auctor in rem suam* where this is expressly sanctioned by the truster, who appoints the trustee having foreseen the conflict of interest, or where all the beneficiaries or potential beneficiaries give their free and informed consent to a transaction: *Buckner* v *Jopp's Trs* (1887). Express sanction will typically arise where the truster specifies that a trustee may receive remuneration for carrying out his function, since otherwise this would fall foul of the principle.

There has been some debate as to whether the truster must expressly make clear in the trust deed that the trustee or trustees are authorised to do something in breach of the principle or whether this may be inferred in certain circumstances. But there is authority that implied authorisation may be inferred from terms of the trust: for example, *Goodsir* v *Carruthers* (1858); *Sarris* v *Clark* (1995). Any such authorisation in the trust deed will be strictly interpreted by the courts and will permit the trustee to do no more than was clearly intended by the truster. Therefore, the truster should make his intention clear and, preferably, should expressly state any circumstances in which the trustee is authorised act to their personal benefit.

Where there is no authority from the truster permitting the trustee to act in a way that would otherwise breach the principle *auctor in rem suam*, the court has no power to grant authority. But where a transaction in breach of the principle has taken place, the court does have statutory power to relieve a trustee from personal liability in respect of it, provided that the trustee acted "honestly and reasonably" (s 32 of the Trusts (Scotland) Act 1921).

Finally, there is nothing to prevent a trustee resigning and then entering into transactions with the remaining trustees in regard to the trust estate. But if the resignation took place in order to facilitate a specific transaction that was negotiated when the trustee still held office, it may be subject to challenge: A J P Menzies, *The Law of Scotland affecting Trustees* (2nd edn, 1913), para 502; *Halley's Trs* v *Halley* (1920). The issue is whether the trustee, using their knowledge of the trust estate, may take unfair advantage of the beneficiaries. If there is a challenge, the court will therefore examine carefully any transaction involving ex-trustees which followed soon after the date of resignation and the trustee will have the onus of showing that the transaction was fair, particularly when it was the result of negotiation when the trustee still held office.

There are clear categories of case where a trustee will be in breach of trust as *auctor in rem suam*:

A trustee must not transact with the trust estate

Trustees must not buy trust property or contract to sell their own property (heritable or moveable) to the trust, nor can they borrow from, or lend to, the trust estate. As well as direct transactions, it is possible to challenge indirect transactions if it appears that they were made in order to avoid the rule. So if a trustee agrees with a third party that the latter will purchase trust property and then sell it on to him, it would be possible to seek interdict to prevent the transfer to the trustee or to have it reduced if it had taken place: for example, *Clark* v *Clark's Exrx* (1989).

Likewise, transactions with persons related to trustees may fall foul of the rule that a trustee must not act as *auctor in rem suam*. The underlying idea here is that such transactions will raise suspicion that the trustee will sacrifice his duty to his interest: trustees, with their intimate knowledge of the trust estate, may be suspected of selling trust assets at an undervalue.

Remuneration

The default rule is that trustees are expected to act gratuitously. This means that they are entitled to their out-of-pocket expenses for acting as trustees, but not to anything more. After all, the duty of the trustee is to watch over the interests of the estate which he has accepted into his care and if he could remunerate himself out of the trust estate then he would be in a position where his duty and his interest were in conflict: for example Menzies, para 460; *Lord Gray and Others* (1856). If trustees are to receive a salary, and commonly they do if they are acting as professional trustees, this must be clearly specified by the truster in the trust deed.

Trustees must not make a secret profit

Apart from the question of remuneration, a trustee must not, in general, gain a personal advantage or profit from acting as trustee. As the 18th-century judge Lord Kames put it, if a trustee were permitted to make a profit then "he will soon lose sight of his duty, and direct his management chiefly for making profit to himself" (*Principles of Equity,* II.1, p 335). The only benefit a trustee can legitimately acquire is payment for acting as a trustee but that must have been expressly authorised by the terms of the trust deed.

Actions and defences

Any transaction which takes place where the trustee has a conflict of interest is not void but voidable and for it to be set aside it must be challenged within a reasonable time. The beneficiaries may bring a challenge but can decide simply to acquiesce in the transaction and allow it to stand. Co-trustees have a separate right to challenge, as do any creditors of the trust. If any of these parties consented to the transaction, however, then that is a defence against them should they later seek to reduce it, provided that the consent was informed consent. That means that the party knew it was wrong but condoned it. A third party has no interest to challenge the transaction, but it appears that the truster, if still alive, does have an interest since one of his trustees has failed in his fiduciary duty.

Any trustee who obtains a benefit or property under a transaction that was entered into as *auctor in rem suam* is deemed to hold it in trust for the beneficiaries who may recover it by means of an action of reduction and an action of count, reckoning and payment. It is no defence that the transaction was fair or entered into in good faith. Nor is it a defence that no loss accrued to the trust estate. If there is loss to the trust, the beneficiaries can raise an action of damages to recover this, regardless of whether the transaction was fair or reasonable.

In a few specific instances, the court has been prepared to hold that there is a defence where the transaction was both fair and reasonable. The first relates to a sale to a related person. Although the court will view a sale of trust property to the spouse of a trustee with great suspicion, there is no absolute rule against it and the transaction may stand, for example where the full price was paid and there is no evidence that the trustee benefited personally (as in *Burrell v Burrell's Trs* (1915)). Likewise, a trustee may enter into a transaction with a beneficiary to purchase his interest in the trust, but only where he provides him with full information about the transaction:

Dougan v *Macpherson* (1902). It is important to note that these categories are very restricted. There is limited scope for the court to apply s 32 of the Trusts (Scotland) Act 1921 and relieve a trustee of liability where he has acted honestly and reasonably and ought fairly to be excused. By definition, a trustee who has been *auctor in rem suam* has not acted reasonably.

The trustee has a defence if the truster foresaw the conflict and expressly authorised transactions by the trustee concerned that would otherwise have been in breach of trust. But this authorisation must be in clear terms. Is it enough for a trustee to dissociate himself, for instance by leaving the room, when a decision is made in circumstances where he has a personal conflict of interest? Such an arrangement clearly deprives those interested in the trust of the benefit of that trustee's opinion and advice (which, as a trustee, he is bound to give in the best interests of the trust). However, this course of action may be justified and appropriate. The only other option would be for the trustee to resign as a trustee and, in some cases, it may be impossible to avoid this. The circumstances giving rise to the conflict may be relevant. Where the trustee has voluntarily created a situation where a transaction represents a conflict of interests, it is submitted that there may be a stronger case for him to resign, rather than temporarily step aside from being involved in decision-making, than in circumstances where the conflict arises involuntarily (for example, through an inheritance). This seems to be the logic of the opinion of Lord Inglis in the case of *Perston* v *Perston's Trs* (1863). But the matter is not free from doubt, and the fact that he acted in good faith is no defence to a trustee who is *auctor in rem suam*.

Proper motivation

It is part of his fiduciary duty that a trustee, in any act of trust administration, must take into account the trust purposes and the interests of the beneficiaries. He should not be unduly influenced by personal beliefs, be they moral, ethical, cultural or political, when making decisions as a trustee: for example *Martin v City of Edinburgh District Council* (1988). That would be to place his private beliefs in conflict with the trust purposes as expressed by the truster. Likewise, the trustee is not entitled to guess what a deceased truster, in the light of his own known preferences or circumstances, might have decided to do. Such speculative considerations are not relevant: it is the wording of the trust purposes that counts. Of course, a trustee will have private beliefs, and they may legitimately influence his decisions in regard to the trust provided that any decision taken is made in good faith, in the interests of the beneficiaries and in accordance with trust purposes.

Proposals for reform

The rules might be regarded as overly strict, particularly in circumstances where the trust and the beneficiaries actually benefit from a transaction that was entered into in good faith, albeit in breach of fiduciary duty. An example is the case of *Cherry's Trs* v *Patrick* (1911), where the trustee, who had sold goods to the trust commercially but at a wholesale discount, was held bound to pay all the profits he had made over several years. This was despite the fact that the transactions had been as favourable to the trust as any by an arm's-length supplier would have been. On the other hand, relaxing the rule and condoning the breach of the duty may encourage trustees to abuse their position by entering into such transactions and it would add complication if the court had to investigate all the facts rather than simply apply a prohibition based on a clear rule.

The Scottish Law Commission has proposed (Scot Law Com No 123, 2003, para 4.16) an amendment where the court is satisfied that a transaction by a trustee, in breach of a fiduciary duty, has been of benefit to the trust estate and the beneficiaries as a whole. Provided that the terms of the transaction were at least as favourable to the trust estate as those likely to be contained in a comparable arm's-length transaction, it is proposed that the court be able to relieve the trustees, in whole or in part, of the consequences of the transaction having been in breach of fiduciary duty.

Essential Facts

- Trustees cannot use property for their own benefit and must use it in compliance with trust purposes in the interests of the beneficiaries.
- A trustee is under a general duty of care to exercise the same care and diligence in managing trust property as a person of ordinary prudence would use in the management of their own affairs.
- A trustee must not be *auctor in rem suam* and must not permit his personal interests to conflict with the interests of the trust.
- A trustee must not make a secret profit from the trust and, if he does, is deemed to hold it in trust for the beneficiaries to whom he is accountable.
- A trustee must enter transactions with proper motivation, otherwise he will be in breach of trust and required to account.
- Where there is a breach of fiduciary duty, an action of count, reckoning and payment may be brought by a beneficiary, co-trustee or even the truster; if there is quantifiable loss to the trust estate, an action of damages may be brought as an alternative.

Essential Cases

Martin v City of Edinburgh District Council (1988): the council, responsible for administering 58 trusts, was in 1984 controlled by a party which decided, as a matter of political policy, to withdraw all trust investments in South Africa because of their disapproval of the Government there. This was held to be a breach of trust, since the council members as trustees had failed to consider whether this was in the best interests of the beneficiaries and had failed to seek advice as to what those interests were. Even though the value of the investments increased, the trustees, in pursuance of motives of their own, had ignored their prime duty to the beneficiaries.

Clarke v Clarke's Trs (1925): the trustees were authorised to retain investments which the truster himself had made. Without reviewing the propriety or suitability of those investments, they simply maintained them and some of the shares which the truster had invested in lost their value. This was held to be a breach of trust, since, according to Lord Cullen, trustees must "keep a prudent and business-like eye" upon investments and review them periodically as any ordinarily prudent business person would do.

Melville v Noble's Trs (1896): trustees left a large sum on deposit receipt with a bank for 19 years. They did not give thought to investment during that time and the value of the fund declined. This was held to be a breach of trust since it was the trustees' duty to invest so as to yield an investment return and this they did not do. A person of ordinary prudence would not have failed, as the trustees did, to consider the question of investment and would have sought a higher rate of return than the bank deposit rate.

8 VARIATION OF TRUST PURPOSES

There are many reasons why it might become necessary to vary the original purposes of a trust. The original powers given to the trustees may no longer be adequate for them to continue to meet the trust purposes. Those purposes themselves might no longer be easy, or even possible, to fulfil because of social or legal changes. On the other hand, changes to the purposes or powers of a trust may bring positive benefits, making the administration of the trust easier or fairer, and allowing trustees to take advantage of new developments, for example in the tax regime.

This is an area where reform is likely in the near future. In addition to a Discussion Paper (No 129), the Scottish Law Commission produced a report in 2007 on *Variation and Termination of Trusts*. This contains, in draft form, the Variations of Trusts and Charities (Scotland) Bill which, in this chapter, is referred to as the "Draft Bill".

EXTRAJUDICIAL VARIATION

Where all the beneficiaries in a trust are of full age and capacity, and they consent to a particular course of action being followed which the terms of the trust deed do not prevent, then no-one may object to this course of action being carried out and the court will not prevent it. This is a rule of the common law and the consent of the truster is not required.

In practice, it may be quite rare to have circumstances in which all the beneficiaries are of full age (aged 18 or over), have legal capacity and are willing to consent to a proposed arrangement for the termination or variation of a trust. If these ideal circumstances do not exist, then judicial intervention is required.

Note the following:

- If all the beneficiaries agree, and have the capacity to do so, they can bring the trust to an end or they can vary its purposes (in effect, they can bring it to an end and create a new trust, with the same or different trustees). This is so even though it means ignoring certain directions by the truster – for example, to postpone payment of capital to a later date. The Scottish Law Commission proposes to give statutory effect to this rule (Scot Law Com No 206 (2007), para 4.4).

- Once all the beneficiaries have capacity, the trustees simply have no interest in preventing them doing what they all consent to do.
- If some of the beneficiaries lack capacity, then it is necessary to seek judicial intervention. The court may consent on behalf of such beneficiaries, but it is not bound to do so (see "Judicial variation" below).
- A person aged under 18 cannot assent to variation or termination; but persons aged 18 can do so, provided that they otherwise have legal capacity. Anyone aged 16 or 17 is deemed incapable of assenting but the court must take such account as it thinks proper of the attitude of such a beneficiary to the proposed arrangement (this is the effect of the Age of Legal Capacity (Scotland) Act 1991). This rule, in the current Scottish Law Commission proposals for reform, will be retained. It will also be made explicit that the parent or guardian of a child under the age of 16 cannot consent on the child's behalf to a variation or termination of any trust in which the child has an interest (Scot Law Com No 206 (2007), paras 4.6–4.16). In current practice, court approval is sought in such cases, since there is always a risk that the parent's interests will conflict with those of the child.

JUDICIAL VARIATION OF PRIVATE TRUSTS: THE CURRENT LAW

Recognising the practical difficulties, Parliament provided the court with powers to approve proposed variations in trusts in the Trusts (Scotland) Act 1961. Under s 1(1) the Court of Session has the power to approve any arrangement varying or revoking all or any trust purposes, or enlarging the powers of the trustees. A petition must be brought by the trustees, or any of the beneficiaries (including potential beneficiaries), before the court may exercise this power and it will only do so if it is of the opinion that no prejudice will result to those on whose behalf it is sanctioning the arrangement.

There are three classes of person on whose behalf the court can give approval:

(1) any beneficiary who is unable to assent by reason of any legal disability (including nonage);

(2) any person (whether ascertained or not) who may become a beneficiary at a future date or on the happening of a future event, as being a person of any specified description or a member of any specified class, unless that person was capable of consenting and

would be of that description or class if the date or event had already happened; or

(3) any person unborn (including those *in utero*).

As noted above, a person aged over 16 but who is not yet 18 is deemed incapable of assenting. However, the court will take such account as it thinks appropriate of his attitude to the arrangement.

The second class is complicated, although it is clearly aimed at destinations over in favour of heirs. The rule is that the court may consent for some potential beneficiary if that person is not the actual beneficiary or, at the date when the petition is presented, the person next in line to be the actual beneficiary. This is best demonstrated in an example. Suppose, therefore, that a trust is set up to benefit "A, whom failing B, whom failing C". Assuming that he is of age to do so, A is the beneficiary and must give his own consent to the variation. B must do the same, again if capable of assenting, since B would have become the actual beneficiary if A had already died. But C, who would only become a potential beneficiary on the death of A or B, and the actual beneficiary on the deaths of *both* A and B, may have his consent given by the court. This is regardless of whether C himself is capable of assenting in his own right. In other words, the court cannot consent for the actual beneficiary, or for anyone who, but for a single contingent event, would be the actual beneficiary, but may do so on behalf of anyone more remote.

These provisions are important because they make it easier to create a variation of trust purposes. However, the court has discretion. Simply because a proposed variation is not prejudicial does not mean that the court is bound to grant approval for it. The court has no power to grant consent on behalf of anyone who is legally capable of consenting on his own behalf. Nor can the court second guess such a person: it cannot overrule anyone's valid consent on the basis that the variation is prejudicial to them. A beneficiary is perfectly entitled to withhold consent and, in so doing, prevent any proposed variation from taking effect. Indeed, the common law rule, that the consent of all the beneficiaries who are capable of giving it must be obtained before the variation can take effect, was not affected by the 1961 Act.

When will a transaction be prejudicial? Usually, it will be when it involves some financial detriment for the beneficiaries, although that alone would not be decisive in the presence of relevant competing social or other factors. A variation may often increase or decrease the number of potential beneficiaries and, on the balance of probabilities (which is the relevant standard), that may often involve financial consequences which might be prejudicial.

Even where a beneficiary loses financially by a variation arrangement, however, the court may conceivably still approve it if the loss is more than compensated by other kinds of gain. It is clear that the court has discretion and may refuse a petition even in the absence of any prejudice. Where there is no prejudice, the court is also free to grant a petition, and grant consent, even if this has no effect at all on the beneficiaries (the variation may, for example, simply make life easier for the trustees).

The remote potential beneficiary

Under s 1(6) of the 1961 Act, a "beneficiary" includes "any person having, directly or indirectly, an interest, whether vested or contingent, under the trust". We saw above that the court may consent on behalf of remote beneficiaries if this will not prejudice them. But what if it might prejudice them? The wording of the section is very wide: many people may have a contingent interest in trust property that is so remote there is almost no chance they will qualify to receive any of the property concerned. In *Phillips and Others, Petrs* (1964), the court took the view that s 1(6) could not have been intended to apply to persons whose interest was so remote as to be negligible. Such persons should simply not be regarded as "beneficiaries" within the meaning of the Act. Given the wording of s 1(6), this interpretation is questionable. Jurisprudence relative to Art 1 of the First Protocol to the European Convention on Human Rights suggests that it is likely to be a breach of a beneficiary's human rights for a court to approve a variation that had the effect of removing or diminishing his interest, however remote, in a trust. (The Scottish Law Commission cited, on this point, *James v United Kingdom* (1986).) In the event that a remote possibility does materialise, trustees who have varied the trust purposes may therefore find themselves liable to the remote beneficiary for any loss suffered, particularly since it is not necessarily the case that they could gain adequate insurance cover against the possibility of his claim emerging. On proposed reforms in this area, see below.

Proposals for reform in the variation of private trusts

To avoid doubt, the Commission proposes that the question of whether a transaction is prejudicial be defined quite generously, making clear that this refers to more than mere economic prejudice. This will allow the court to take into account non-economic and other appropriate factors (Draft Bill, s 3(1) and (2)).

The court under the 1961 Act has no power to approve any variation on behalf of an untraceable beneficiary. The trustees can only seek insurance against such a person emerging. If the untraced beneficiary has an interest of negligible value, this will usually pose no difficulty. But where this is not the case, the Commission recommends giving the court power to approve an arrangement to vary the trust on behalf of an untraced beneficiary when it is satisfied (a) that reasonable steps were taken to trace that person and (b) that the arrangement would not be prejudicial to that person's interests. A possible way of avoiding prejudice may be for the trustees, at the time the variation is approved, to be directed to retain a fund equal to the actuarial value of that person's interest in the trust.

The current rule, that the court has no power to consent to any arrangement on behalf of a beneficiary of full age who has capacity, will remain. This is so even where a beneficiary who refuses consent will be unaffected by, or will even benefit from, a proposed variation.

Finally, petitions for termination and variation under s 1 of the 1961 Act are currently heard in the Inner House of the Court of Session before three Lords of Council and Session. The judges themselves have recommended a change so that such cases may be heard in the Outer House before a single judge, who will have power to remit cases of particular difficulty to the Inner House (Discussion Paper on *Trustees and Trust Administration* (Scot Law Com No 126, 2004), para 5.18).

The remote potential beneficiary: reform

The Commission has proposed that the court should be able to relieve trustees of potential liability in circumstances where prejudice results to very remote beneficiaries. It has differentiated between (a) those whose right is highly contingent, for example where their status as an actual beneficiary will only materialise in the unlikely event that a number of people pre-decease them; and (b) the situation where an interest might emerge, but is very unlikely to do so, for example through the birth of a child to an aged truster. The court, it is proposed, will have the power to approve a variation, even a potentially prejudicial one, if satisfied that the beneficiary's interest is of negligible value. If it does so, the trustees will be relieved of liability to any beneficiary whose interest was determined to be of negligible value but which subsequently emerged (Draft Bill, s 4). In the case of the child whose birth is very unlikely, provided it is of opinion that there is no reasonable likelihood of the interest coming into existence, the court will have power to approve a variation notwithstanding the possibility of prejudice to an unborn or unascertained person (Draft Bill, s 3(2)).

Alimentary trusts

The truster may declare an interest in the trust to be "alimentary". No specific form of words is necessary, but the essence is that the income of the trust, usually by way of liferent or annuity, is to be used for the support and maintenance of the beneficiary (who will usually be a young, elderly or otherwise vulnerable person) or, in addition, to pay for his education. Since financial support is of the essence, the liferent cannot be excessive in amount; it should be a sum that is reasonable, taking into account the beneficiary's circumstances. If the rationale of the provision no longer applies, for instance if it was established to pay for full-time education which has ended, then the liferent will cease to be alimentary. If it is excessive, the excess (the amount above what is reasonably necessary for support) may be arrested by the beneficiary's creditors. Otherwise, two important general rules apply:

(1) once he has begun enjoying an alimentary interest under the trust, the beneficiary cannot renounce it or assign it to someone else; and

(2) the right cannot be arrested by the beneficiary's creditors except to the extent that instalments have fallen due. Therefore, future income from the fund cannot be arrested.

Since the beneficiary cannot renounce his interest once he has entered into the enjoyment of it, there are, in the current law, special rules under s 1(4) of the 1961 Act for the variation or revocation of an alimentary provision. The court must be satisfied:

• that the proposed arrangement is "reasonable" having regard to the beneficiary's income and any other material factors; and

• the alimentary beneficiary consents or, if he is incapable of consenting, the court approves the arrangement on his behalf.

Taking into account material factors entitles the court to examine the effect of the variation on the fiars. In practice, the court will also require that the consent of the fiars be obtained. These rules are substantially re-enacted in the Commission's Draft Bill.

JUDICIAL VARIATION OF PUBLIC TRUSTS: THE CURRENT LAW

It is important here to remember the difference between a public trust and a charitable trust. Not every public trust is charitable. A public trust is simply one that is intended to benefit the public or a section thereof. The Charities and Trustee Investment (Scotland) Act 2005 has set up a regime for the regulation of charities in Scotland. While some trusts may be charitable, the 2005 Act is best thought of as dealing with registered charities, ie charities which appear in the Scottish Charities Register. It is important not to confuse public trusts with those bodies which meet the "charity" test by fulfilling charitable purposes such as the advancement of religion, and public trusts. It is possible to set up a registered charity that would not meet the requirements for the creation of a public trust. If it is not registered as a charity, and there is no requirement to do so, then a public trust, at the moment, is unaffected by the Office of the Scottish Charity Regulator. This may change if effect is given to the Scottish Law Commission's current proposals (see below).

Although, in theory, the rule that beneficiaries may terminate a trust or vary its terms if they unanimously consent to do so might have application in public trusts, and indeed the Trusts (Scotland) Act 1961 also applies to both private and public trusts, in practice the consent of all potential beneficiaries would usually be impossible to achieve and it is not a route adopted for varying or terminating public trusts.

The *nobile officium* and the *cy-près* doctrine

At common law, a petition may be made to the *nobile officium* of the Court of Session in order to prevent the lapse of a public trust. The court may grant an equitable remedy to save the trust. Where a testator demonstrates an intention to make a gift to charity, but omits to describe how this gift is to be put into effect, then the court may supply these details and give effect to the intention. Since the intention is one that can and will be fulfilled, this is not an example of the *cy-près* doctrine, the basis of which permits the Court of Session, on equitable grounds, to order that trust funds be applied in a manner as close as possible to that intended by the truster where, for some reason, effect cannot directly be given to the truster's expressed intention.

The court may sanction a *cy-près* scheme (sometimes referred to as an "approximation scheme"), but can do so only in fairly narrow circumstances. The Lord Ordinary in the Outer House (or, if he remits the matter, the judges in the Inner House) will authorise such a scheme when it is equitable to do so in circumstances where the trust purposes have become impossible or particularly inappropriate in their current form. Where the purposes are no longer appropriate, the court may sanction some change to another, but similar, purpose. There are many potential variants in which the court might be asked to approve a *cy-près* scheme: for example, a trust may be set up with more funds than are necessary for its purposes, in which case the excess funds may be diverted to some similar purpose; or too few funds may exist to meet the purposes, in which case these may be replaced by more modest, yet similar, purposes.

A *cy-près* scheme can only be used in restricted circumstances in order to vary the purpose of a public trust. It cannot be used in the following cases, for example:

- where the truster himself has made provision in the trust deed for what is to be done if the trust should fail;
- where the trust purposes are void (for *cy-près* to work, the purpose must be valid but, for some reason, impossible or inappropriate);
- where the trustees have performed acts that were *ultra vires* (this is a defect the court will not correct using *cy-près*); or
- where the original purposes are so unique that there is nothing that could approximate to them.

Even where it can be used, the court has discretion not to use it.

Impossibility need not be absolute. There can be no general rule as to the degree to which the functioning of the trust must be hampered before the doctrine will apply. It depends on the precise facts of each case and the approach taken by the court has been stricter in some cases than others. However, it is clear that strong or compelling expediency is sufficient to justify the exercise of the doctrine: *MacDonald Trs, Petrs* (2009).

Whether the court will give effect to a *cy-près* scheme depends on the nature of the problem faced by the trustees since a distinction is drawn between initial failure of trust purposes and subsequent failure.

Initial failure

This is where the purposes of a public trust are impossible from the beginning and the trust cannot be put into operation. In these circumstances the truster and his heirs retain an interest, since ownership of the trust property, for want of any other option, might revert to them. This is known as a resulting trust. This will not happen where the truster demonstrated "a general charitable intention" in setting up the trust, since this indicates that the truster did not intend the property to be returned to him or to his heirs. In such a case the property will be applied to purposes as near as possible to those prescribed by the truster.

A general charitable intention is one which is aimed at providing a benefit to the public, rather than an intention to benefit any specific charitable institution. The aim must be to benefit a cause, such as the relief of poverty or the welfare of children. It is one thing to leave a house to be maintained as a memorial hospital, and another to direct that it may be sold and the proceeds to be spent for improving a local hospital. In the former case, *Hay's JF* v *Hay's Trs* (1952), the intention of leaving a mansion house in Shetland to be maintained as a memorial was held to be so integral to the bequest that there was no general charitable intention, even though the trustees had discretion over the class of persons in Shetland to be cared for within the proposed institution. The bequest failed because of lack of funds and, in the circumstances, it was held that there was no basis for a *cy-près* scheme to operate. If the house could have been sold to provide funds to further the charitable purpose of assisting a certain class of local persons in need of help, then a *cy-près* scheme would have been possible. The wording of the bequest, therefore, is of central importance. If the wording indicates the desire to benefit class X (for example, poor children) through organisation Y, much depends on whether the court can infer from the words used the general intention to benefit X or the particular intention to promote Y in doing so.

So long as it is possible to help local people in the way identified, a general charitable intention is not lost by specifying a locality. However, a bequest to provide support to the operators of lifeboats in a landlocked area where there are no lifeboats, and no need for any, would not be saved by a *cy-près* scheme if the local area nominated is an essential part of the bequest. Similarly, if a testator wishes to benefit a particular charitable institution and, at the time of her death, that institution no longer exists, then the bequest lapses unless a general charitable intention has been evinced. If the institution exists but has merely changed its name, then the trust will still operate. If it has never existed, the wording might be read as indicating a general charitable intention even though the intention was to benefit a particular (non-existent) organisation. The situation is more complicated if the institution has amalgamated or, in the case of a church for example, a part has seceded from the whole. Determining to whom the benefit should be given would be a matter of interpretation in each case.

The Scottish Law Commission has proposed that, in future, where the court finds that a general charitable intention exists, it should have the power to remit to the Office of the Scottish Charity Regulator (OSCR) to consider whether, for example, the public trust set up would meet the "charity" test. This would presumably be done only when an application for registration as a charity is likely to be made in future. Otherwise, there is no proposal to change the operation of the court's power to approve a *cy-près* scheme. Other reform proposals are discussed at the end of this chapter.

Supervening failure

This arises where the trust initially operates successfully but, for some reason, its capacity for continued operation is in doubt. The truster in these circumstances is clearly divested of ownership in the trust property and there is no possibility of a resulting trust in favour of his estate. A general charitable intention is not required in order for the court to approve a *cy-près* scheme. As long as the truster has not provided for the subsequent failure of trust purposes using a destination over, then a *cy-près* scheme can be used. Whether it will be used clearly depends on what is meant by "failure" of the trust purposes.

It is not enough that carrying out the trust purposes has become more difficult for the trustees. Nor is it enough that the class of beneficiaries has grown considerably smaller since the trust was created. It must be the case that, owing to changed circumstances, the trust purposes can no longer be given effect in the way envisaged by the truster and that strong or compelling expediency justifies a change. As mentioned above, the court has varied in the strictness of its approach to determining whether trust purposes have failed. It is possible to compare the approach of the judges in *Scotstown Moor Children's Camp* (1948) with that in *Glasgow YMCA Trs, Petrs* (1934).

STATUTORY VARIATION OF PUBLIC TRUSTS

In addition to the common law jurisdiction, s 9 of the Law Reform (Miscellaneous Provisions) (Scotland) Act 1990 provides both the Court of Session and the sheriff court with powers to approve a scheme for the variation of trust purposes in any public trust. The Act is an alternative to a petition to the *nobile officium* and there is a degree of overlap between the two procedures. An application under statute should be a quicker and cheaper option. A separate scheme under s 10, aimed at small public trusts, is intended to be even simpler.

Section 9(1) lists the circumstances in which the power may be exercised, allowing the court to approve a scheme for the variation or re-organisation of trust purposes if it is satisfied:

- that the purposes of the trust have been fulfilled as far as is possible or can no longer be given effect to; or
- that the purposes of the trust provide a use for only part of the trust property; or
- that the purposes of the trust were expressed by reference to an area which has ceased to have effect for these purposes or a class of persons or area which has ceased to be suitable or appropriate for the trust; or

- that the purposes of the trust have been adequately provided for by other means, or have ceased to be such as would enable the trust to be entered in the Scottish Charity Register or have otherwise ceased to provide a suitable and effective method of using the trust property, having regard to the spirit of the trust deed.

Before it can approve any scheme, the court (under s 9(2)) must be satisfied that the proposed variation will enable the trust's resources to be applied to better effect consistently with the spirit of the trust deed, having regard to changes in social and economic conditions since the trust was constituted.

Every application must be intimated to the Lord Advocate, who may enter appearance as a party in the public interest (s 9(6)). Where an application is made to the sheriff, this should, under s 9(5), be in the sheriffdom with which the trust has its closest connection or, failing that, in the sheriffdom where any of the trustees resides. In the absence of either possibility, it must be raised before the sheriff of Lothian and Borders in Edinburgh.

SMALL PUBLIC TRUSTS

The 1990 Act regards a public trust as small where its annual income does not exceed £5,000. This figure may be amended by the Secretary of State under s 10(15). The four grounds of variation are the same as in s 9. The difference is that the court is not involved. A majority of the trustees, if they are of the opinion that one of the grounds exists, may, under s 10(2):

(a) modify the trust purposes (this, under s 10(3), can be effected by a simple resolution);
(b) transfer the assets to another public trust; or
(c) amalgamate the trust with one or more public trusts.

In regard to (b) and (c), the other trust involved must have purposes that are not dissimilar in character to those set out in the original trust deed: s 10(8).

The majority, in passing the resolution, are required:

(a) to have regard, where the trust purposes relate to a particular locality, to the circumstances of that locality (s 10(5)(a) and (9)(a));
(b) to have regard to the extent to which it may be desirable to achieve economy by amalgamating two or more of the trusts (s 10(5)(b)); and
(c) to ascertain that the trustees of the trust to which it is proposed to transfer the assets will consent to the transfer (s 10(9)(c)).

An amalgamation or transfer of assets will be effective 2 months after the proper advertisement of the resolution (s 10(12) and (13)). The Lord Advocate has power to intervene under s 10(14) and prevent the modification, transfer of assets or amalgamation, if it appears to him that such a variation should not proceed. At common law, any person having an interest may seek to reduce the resolution on cause shown.

Finally, s 11 deals with trusts with an annual income not exceeding £1,000 in which the trustees have no power under the trust deed to expend the capital of the trust. If they act unanimously, the trustees may, under s 11, having first advertised the fact, expend capital provided that they are satisfied (a) that the income of the trust is too small to achieve trust purposes and (b) that there is no reasonable prospect of a transfer of assets under s 10 or that the expenditure of capital is more likely to achieve the trust's purposes. Again, the Lord Advocate may intervene by asking the court to prohibit this if it proceeds on insufficient grounds.

PROPOSALS FOR REFORM

The Charities and Trustee Investment (Scotland) Act 2005 set up a new regime for the regulation of charities in Scotland. A public trust which is set up for charitable purposes is not subject to this regime unless it becomes a registered charity. Provisions under the 2005 Act (ss 39–42) deal with the approval of re-organisation schemes involving registered charities. These were largely framed on the model of the 1990 Act, but the key difference is that the court is not involved. Instead, approval must be sought from the Office of the Scottish Charity Regulator (OSCR). There is the possibility of an appeal to the Scottish Charity Appeals Panel, rather than the courts. Under s 40(1) of the 2005 Act the OSCR, of its own accord or on the application of the charity trustees, may apply to the Court of Session for approval of a scheme.

The Scottish Law Commission regards the current law as unsatisfactory. It aims to introduce a single set of criteria for the re-organisation of public trusts. It has also proposed that the OSCR in future should take on the additional responsibility for approving the variation of public trusts that are not charities (Report on *Variation and Termination of Trusts* (Scot Law Com, 2007), paras 6.18 and 6.25–6.26; Draft Bill, ss 9 and 10).

Rather than the existing criteria under the 1990 and 2005 Acts, for public trusts and charities respectively, a simpler set of criteria has been proposed. This is that the OSCR should have the power to approve a scheme of re-organisation, when it is satisfied:

(a) that the scheme will enable the trust's resources to be applied to better effect consistently with the spirit of its constitution, having regard to changes in social and economic conditions since the trust was constituted; and

(b) that in doing so, the OSCR should have special regard, where appropriate, to:

(i) the interest of any locality with which the trust is closely connected; and

(ii) the possibility of effecting economy in administration by amalgamating two or more trusts.

These proposals do not represent a major departure in principle, but they do mean an expanded role for the OSCR which will no longer deal simply with registered charities. As things stand, it will still be possible, as at present, for the OSCR to apply to the Court of Session for approval of a scheme.

The proposal to expand the OSCR may reflect dissatisfaction with the development of the law in regard to educational endowments which currently falls under the Education (Scotland) Act 1980. Such endowments, when they are governed by a registered charity, have since 2006 had to apply to the OSCR to approve schemes of re-organisation. Those not governed by a charity must currently still use the approval mechanism set up under the 1980 legislation. There is no clear principled reason why this should be so, and if the proposals are enacted there will be uniformity of approach.

Essential Facts

- Trust purposes can be varied by the beneficiaries at common law provided that they all consent.
- The court has statutory powers to consent on behalf of beneficiaries who are unable to do so, but cannot override the decision of a beneficiary who does not consent.
- The court can only consent on behalf of beneficiaries to a variation in a private trust where no prejudice will result to those beneficiaries from that variation.
- The Court of Session has an equitable jurisdiction at common law to vary the purposes of a public trust in circumstances of strong and compelling expediency and to approve a *cy-près* scheme to put in place similar purposes where it is possible to approximate the original ones.

- Where there is initial failure of a trust, a *cy-près* scheme is the sole remedy and it can only be granted where the truster has evinced a general charitable intention.
- A statutory procedure exists for the sheriff court, or Court of Session, to vary the purposes of an existing public trust in certain circumstances where there is supervening hindrance in carrying out those purposes. Any variation must enable the trust's resources to be applied to better effect consistent with the spirit of the trust's constitution.
- Small public trusts, with income below £5,000 annually, are subject to less formal procedures allowing a majority of trustees, in defined circumstances, to re-organise them extrajudicially.
- The Lord Advocate may act for the public interest and object to the re-organisation of a public trust.
- The procedure for re-organising a trust is not currently the same as that for reorganising a registered charity, although there are proposals to bring these procedures into greater uniformity. These will not affect the common law position.

Essential Cases

Glasgow Royal Infirmary v Magistrates of Glasgow (1888): a society raised funds to build a home connected to the Royal Infirmary in Glasgow for patients convalescing from fever. The town council later established a hospital for fever patients who were no longer placed in the Infirmary. The court, in dealing with the assets in the fund that were left over, was faced with having to determine how best to give effect to the wishes of those who raised the fund. The Infirmary sought to use the money to provide a home for nurses employed there. The magistrates sought to apply the funds to assist convalescent fever patients in the Glasgow Fever Hospital. The court authorised the latter scheme on the basis that it was closer to the original intention which was to benefit a particular class of person, ie those convalescing from fever. It was made clear that the patients to be assisted must be in Glasgow and the fund could not be applied elsewhere.

Scotstown Moor Children's Camp (1948): a camp near Aberdeen was established to provide a short holiday for "needy and ailing children". Because of the outbreak of war in 1939, the camp was discontinued and some of its buildings were requisitioned by the Air Ministry (and remained so until 1947). One building was destroyed by fire in 1945, the capacity to receive food donations was affected by rationing and private donations had fallen off while the camp lay dormant. The trustees sought approval of a *cy-près* scheme by which the trust's assets would be transferred to the Boys' Brigade in Aberdeen. The court held that it did not have general discretion to divert funds from one object to another. The object, to provide a holiday in the country for needy children, was not impossible and the circumstances here did not amount to failure of the trust purposes. Therefore, the court had no jurisdiction to intervene in this case. A narrow construction of "impossibility" was adopted in this case, perhaps influenced by the failure of the trustees to make an attempt to give effect to the trust purposes after the war.

Glasgow YMCA Trs, Petrs (1934): the YMCA in Glasgow had considerable capital but was running an annual revenue deficit. The trust could have continued in this situation for a period of time, but not without risk to its ability to meet the purposes in its trust deed in the long term. Therefore the trustees sought approval of a *cy-près* scheme allowing them to pay off the revenue deficit from the capital fund. The court held that the long-term threat was sufficient to justify its intervention in this case, even though there was presently no impossibility of carrying out the trust purposes.

Phillips, Petrs (1964): a petitioner under s 1 of the 1961 Act sought authorisation of an arrangement to vary a trust set up under a will and codicil which provided for half the residue of an estate to be paid to the surviving issue of the testator's children at the date of death of his last surviving child, whom failing to a variety of remote relations and charitable organisations. The children and their adult issue sought to adjust this while protecting the remote potential beneficiaries by insurance. The court held that the petition need not be served on the remoter beneficiaries and that insurance was unnecessary, since their ultimate interest was so remote and negligible that they did not qualify as beneficiaries under the Act, and no provision need be made for them in the re-organisation scheme. The Act did not intend the court to give consent on behalf of such remote potential beneficiaries.

9 REMEDIES AND THIRD-PARTY RIGHTS

TRUSTEES AND THIRD PARTIES

While administering the trust and carrying out trust purposes, trustees may incur obligations to third parties. Depending on the powers available to them, they may engage in acts such as the buying and selling or exchange of property, borrowing money, granting leases, servitudes or rights in security. In what circumstances can they defend, against third parties, rights which they have in their capacity as joint owners of trust property? In what circumstances will trustees be personally liable to fulfil obligations to third parties? What effect might these obligations have on the trust and the interests of the beneficiaries? To answer these questions it is best to distinguish between obligations entered into with third parties that are within the powers of the trustees (*intra vires*) in terms of powers granted expressly in a trust deed or powers implied under the Trusts (Scotland) Act 1921, and those which are entered into which are not within their powers (*ultra vires*). Before doing so, it is important to distinguish clearly between real rights and personal rights.

REAL RIGHTS AND PERSONAL RIGHTS

A real right is a right *in rem* – that is, a right directly in a thing. The thing can be any kind of property, just as a trust estate can comprise any kind of property. It might be a motor car or a house or an incorporeal right, such as shares in a company or the right to receive the proceeds of a policy of life assurance. Since the right is directly in a thing, it may be defended against anyone. The most important real right is the right of ownership, but a secured creditor has a real right (a right of security) directly in an item of property belonging to his debtor. The right in security is a *jus in re aliena*: a right in a thing foreign to him (ie a right in property owned by another). Therefore, there may be several real rights, held by different people, in the same property: A may own a house; B may have a right in security in A's house in respect of a debt owed to him by A; and C may be a tenant who has a lease (which may have been constituted as a real right) in A's house. In the context of a trust, trustees own trust property and, unless the trust deed prohibits this, they also have the power to grant real rights to others in that property.

A personal right is a right *in personam*, that is, a right enforceable against a person or a limited class of persons. It is not a right directly in a thing and it cannot be exercised against the world at large. Personal rights feature prominently in the law of contract, for example. A buyer has a right to receive the seller's title and places himself under a corresponding duty to pay the price, while the seller has a duty to convey his title but enjoys the right to receive the price. The seller has a personal right against the buyer and vice versa. In general, such rights may be exercised only by the parties to the contract. So if trustees enter into a contract to sell trust property, they can enforce that only against the buyer and he can enforce his right only against them.

A beneficiary has a personal right which can be enforced only against the trustees. The right of a beneficiary in a trust, however, is special because of the rule that it prevails over the rights of the trustee's personal creditors. The beneficiary has a right against the trustee to have the trust purposes carried out and the trust estate preserved or, as the case may be, conveyed to him as sole beneficiary or one of several beneficiaries. That right continues, even if the trustee's personal estate is sequestrated. The personal creditors of a trustee, in the event that the trustee is unable to pay his debts, can recover what is owed from the trustee's personal patrimony through a process of bankruptcy. They have no remedy at all, however, in respect of the trust patrimony which is preserved inviolate. Only creditors of the trust can recover trust property in satisfaction of debt and, in that case, the debt must have been incurred properly by the trustees in their administration of the trust. If it were incurred improperly, then the trustees, in breach of trust, would incur personal liability to make good any loss to the trust estate on a joint and several basis.

THE PERSONAL LIABILITY OF A TRUSTEE

A trustee may be personally liable in an obligation entered into with a third party in two circumstances:

- where the trustee fails to disclose that he is acting in his capacity as a trustee with the intention of binding the trust estate, rather than his personal patrimony. This transaction, though *intra vires*, is one which is entered improperly from the perspective of the trustee;
- where the trustee, in entering the obligation, carries out an act he is not entitled to do in terms of his powers then this will be a breach of trust for which he will be personally liable to the beneficiaries. This transaction, from the perspective of the trustee, will be *ultra vires*.

OBLIGATIONS ENTERED INTO IMPROPERLY

Trustees contracting with a third party in good faith, and within the powers conferred on them by the truster or the law generally, will attract personal liability on the contract unless it is made clear to a third party that he is dealing with them in their capacity as trustees. This is because the third party is entitled to rely on the appearance of things and the apparent creditworthiness of the individual with whom he is dealing. If he has no notice that he is in fact dealing with property held in trust, then the law allows him to recover for any breach of contract against a trustee's personal estate, rather than the trust patrimony.

If the trustees wish to avoid placing their personal patrimony at hazard, they should make it clear that they intend to bind the trust patrimony. To escape personal liability, it is not enough for a trustee to describe himself as a trustee; it must be made clear that the intention is to limit liability to the trust estate only. This means trustees should, in general, clearly state that they are acting "as trustees" or "*qua* trustees". Even then, the presumption of personal liability may not be rebutted unless it is clear in all the circumstances that the third party knew the intention was to bind the trust patrimony only.

If it is clear from the terms of the transaction that the trustees have no personal liability, then the third party can recover damages only to the extent of the value of the trust estate. Since the trust estate can be made subject to such liability, it is logically and legally possible for a trust patrimony to become insolvent. Under s 6(1)(a) of the Bankruptcy (Scotland) Act 1954, a trust estate may, in appropriate circumstances, be sequestrated by creditors of the trust.

LIABILITY

Where the trustees have succeeded in binding the trust patrimony alone, then the creditor in the obligation has only a right of action against the trustees for the time being. A trustee who has resigned, or the estate of one who has died, is not liable for the debt. The trustees for the time being, however, are jointly and severally liable to the extent of the trust patrimony the administration of which they share.

Where one trustee incurs personal liability this cannot be transmitted to his co-trustees unless they have authorised him to act on their behalf in creating the liability. So if trustee T transacts with third party P, and does not tell P that he is acting as a trustee with the intention of binding the trust estate only, P may hold T personally liable on the contract. However, the co-trustees would not usually be liable unless they approved the contract in advance or subsequently ratified and adopted it. If the trustees have employed an agent or manager to carry out administrative tasks, they may incur personal liability for the actions of their agent.

THE TRUSTEE'S RIGHT OF RELIEF

A trustee who has properly entered into a contract as a trustee, and thus exempted himself from personal liability, is entitled to recover all of the personal charges and expenses which he incurred in the process. This is not simply a case of a right to reimbursement. This is a debt on the trust patrimony and the trustee is entitled to expend trust funds in meeting his own expenses before he need resort to his own pocket. A creditor, therefore, seeking payment for these expenses, can recover them from the trust estate if the trustee is personally unable to pay them. This is known as a relief of obligation. The trust estate can be used first to satisfy such debts; it is only if it proves insufficient that the trustee must bear the expense of doing so personally: *Cuningham* v *Montgomerie* (1879).

LEGAL POLICY

The trustee has an advantage over the third party in knowing the financial details of the trust. At least, he ought to know these details and, in law, he is deemed to know them. This is significant in two respects. First, if he incurs expenses which the trust patrimony cannot afford to meet, he must pay them himself. His co-trustees are not liable for them unless they specifically authorised the expenditure. This is because he ought to have incurred them in the knowledge that the trust funds might not cover the value of the expenses (which might include sums owed to third parties). Second, since the trustee is presumed to know the value of the trust fund, the law regards him as offering an implied warranty to a third party. In effect, the law regards him as representing that the fund at his disposal is adequate to meet the obligation he has undertaken. Therefore if the fund is inadequate, he is personally liable to the third party.

ULTRA VIRES TRANSACTIONS

The issue here is not the capacity in which trustees enter into an obligation with a third party, but the question of whether they had the power to enter into the obligation. If the truster specifies that the trustees have no power to sell heritable property, for example, then the trustees will be personally liable if they enter into an obligation to do so. That does not mean, however, that the transaction itself will be void or that any title that passes in consequence of it will be invalid. The law again gives protection to third parties. This time, it does so under statute.

Section 2 of the Trusts (Scotland) Act 1961 provides this protection in relation to the powers listed under s 4(1) of the Trusts (Scotland) Act 1921 in paras (a)–(eb) of that subsection. (Powers 1–6 are listed on page 50.) These are the default powers which all trustees have unless the trust deed specifies otherwise. Therefore, so far as the law is concerned, these are the powers third parties are entitled to assume trustees have unless the trustees specifically tell them otherwise. Section 2 makes any transaction resulting from the use of these powers valid and unchallengeable either by the third party or by any other person on the ground that the act in question was at variance with the terms or purposes of the trust.

The following should be noted.

- Section 2 protects only third parties. The trustees will be personally liable for breach of trust to the beneficiaries and their co-trustees and the beneficiaries will ultimately suffer any loss to the trust patrimony that the trustees personally lack the means to compensate. Such loss should be limited, since the transactions in which third parties are protected are onerous ones involving some return to the trust fund. If a heritable asset is sold by the trustees acting *ultra vires*, the proceeds will enter the trust patrimony and so, while there is a clear breach of trust, the beneficiaries should not be financially prejudiced.

- Third parties do not include co-trustees or beneficiaries (there is no rationale for protecting transactions involving the latter groups, since they should know the terms of the trust deed).

- Section 2 is aimed at ensuring the validity of certain transactions and any legal title derived from them. It does not afford absolute protection. If a third party is party to a fraud with the trustees – for example if they agree to sell trust assets for a sum considerably under their market value – the title will be unchallengeable but the third party will be vulnerable to an action of damages for fraud.

- If the obligation is entered into using a power other than the six referred to in the legislation, it will not be protected.

- The protection is only against challenges on the ground that the act was at variance with the terms or purposes of the trust. A challenge against the transaction on any other ground may succeed (for example, one based on the lack of capacity of a trustee who has become insane).

Section 2 does not require good faith on the part of the trustees or the third party. Therefore a party who purchases trust property, in circumstances where the trustees are prohibited by the trust deed from selling it, will always obtain a title that cannot be challenged on the basis of the prohibition in the trust deed. This is true even if that party was aware of the prohibition at the time of the sale. While this is a considerable protection for the third party, who need not prove good faith, the powers whose exercise triggers s 2 all involve transactions (selling, letting, borrowing on security, exchanging, investing and buying heritable property) which do not necessarily involve any loss to the trust patrimony. If the trustees were giving away trust property, such gratuitous transactions would be subject to challenge.

THIRD-PARTY RIGHTS

As we have seen, the law preserves against challenge certain *ultra vires* transactions entered into by trustees. However, if the trustees, having entered into an *ultra vires* transaction, then find themselves in breach of contract, the third party would have a contractual remedy against them personally but no direct remedy against the trust estate. This is because the trustees could not bind the trust estate to the transaction, since the transaction itself was beyond their powers. Again, they are deemed to know that it was beyond their powers and they are personally liable for choosing to enter into it nonetheless. The contract itself may be valid, if it is of a type that is protected under s 2. What is missing is any right of relief, on the part of the trustees, against the trust estate. Even if the trustees purport in the transaction to bind the trust estate, they cannot do so because they are acting *ultra vires*.

The third party's protection under s 2 does not extend beyond placing the validity of the transaction beyond challenge. In particular, it does not grant the third party a remedy directly against the trust patrimony. All he has is a remedy against the trustees who are not entitled to protect themselves by having recourse to the assets of the trust. The law here chooses to protect the beneficiaries of the trust. This may be to the potential detriment of the third party, if he cannot recover in full from the trustees, although it is the trustees who should ultimately bear the loss. It would be an additional breach of trust for them to use trust assets to pay damages for breach of a contract which it was *ultra vires* for them to enter into. They would be liable to make good the loss to the trust estate at the instance of the beneficiaries.

PROPOSALS FOR REFORM

The Scottish Law Commission has set forward proposals for reform of the law in this area (Discussion Paper on *Liability of Trustees to Third Parties* (Scot Law Com, No 138, 2008)). It has suggested an amendment to s 2(1) of the Trusts (Scotland) Act 1961, extending the protection it offers beyond the categories of transaction protected within the present law. All onerous transactions relating to the trust estate between the trustees and a third party should, it argues, be beyond challenge on the ground that the transaction was at variance with the terms and purposes of the trust. While transactions with trustees will continue to be exempt from protection, a transaction with a third party who is a beneficiary might be protected in future. The difference is that a trustee ought to know the state of trust accounts whereas a beneficiary may be in a weaker position and should not be expected to investigate to the same degree. Protection under s 2(1) does not depend on good faith and, on balance, the Commission seems to have tended to the view that this rule, which has proved workable, should not be changed.

DELICTUAL LIABILITY

There are few reported cases of delictual liability for trustees in Scots law and those that do exist generally relate to delicts committed in the course of a business carried on by trustees. The general rule is that if a business is an asset in the trust, and the trustees carry on that business, then they will be personally liable for delicts committed by them or their agents in the course of the business. However, they will have a right of relief against the trust patrimony and only if that is insufficient will they actually have to make up any shortfall personally.

Much depends on how they are sued. If decree is given against trustees "as trustees", then recovery can only be made from the trust estate and there will be no personal liability: *Mulholland* v *Macfarlane's Trs* (1928). If decree is against the trustees as individuals, then there is no limit; recovery will be made against the trust patrimony with any balance still owing being recovered from the trustees' personal patrimonies.

The Scottish Law Commission has indicated that the issue in regard to delictual liability is the extent to which it is appropriate to permit pursuers, injured by delicts committed by trustees or their agents, to recover damages against trustees personally rather than the trust estate (Scot Law Com No 138 (2008), para 3.6). As well as the trustees as a body being at fault, any individual trustee against whom a claim is made based on his personal fault will be liable to pay damages from his private patrimony (Scot Law Com No 148 (2011), para 3.11). It is further proposed that the body of trustees and any individual trustee who is personally at fault should each have a right of relief against the other, that right being subject to the power of apportionment in s 3(1) of the Law Reform (Miscellaneous Provisions) (Scotland) Act 1940 (Scot Law Com No 148 (2011), para 3.13).

REFORM OF DELICTUAL LIABILITY

The Commission has proposed abandoning the general rule that trustees are personally liable for the delictual acts of their employees or agents. Instead, it has proposed a rule whereby damages should only be payable from a trustee's private patrimony where the trustee is personally at fault. Otherwise, where in the administration of a trust any third party suffers loss from an act or omission of the trustees, or any person for whom they are responsible, damages should in general only be recoverable from the trust patrimony.

EXECUTION OF DEEDS

Is a deed granted by some trustees valid or may it be challenged if not subscribed by all the trustees or a quorum of them? This is a question which affects the security of third-party rights and the law is not entirely satisfactory. The relevant issue is whether a formal deed granted in pursuance of a decision validly taken by a quorum of trustees, such as a decision to grant a heritable security, must be executed by all the trustees (as joint owners of the trust estate) or simply by the quorum. Currently, the law is contained in s 7 of the Trusts (Scotland) Act 1921. This provides that where a deed bears to be granted by the trustees under the trust, its validity cannot be challenged on the ground of procedural irregularity when it is, in fact, executed only by a quorum of trustees.

This provision relates to the difference between decision making, which in general is by a quorum of trustees, and the execution of any deed granted by trustees once the decision has been made. Since all the trustees are joint owners of trust property, it might have been presumed that all must participate in conveying that property to a third party. Section 7 makes it clear that a deed, such as a disposition of heritable property, will not be challenged if granted by a quorum of trustees on the grounds (a) that not all trustees were consulted; or (b) that not all consented; or (c) that any other omission or irregularity of procedure occurred in relation to granting the deed. This is subject to the following qualifications. First, it does not apply if the deed is granted in favour of a beneficiary or a co-trustee. Such a deed would remain challengeable on the grounds stated. Second, the third party must have dealt with the trustees onerously and in good faith.

However, s 7 has raised some doubts so far as the Commisssion is concerned (Scot Law Com No 138 (2008), para 2.46) particularly in relation to the meaning of "good faith" in this context. In its view, a deed should be in the names of all the acting trustees but should require to be signed only by a majority of them in order to be formally valid. This rule would not prejudice the right of trustees to delegate administrative tasks (including the execution of deeds) to agents. An extension of the protection of s 7 has also been suggested as a reform. Protection of third parties, even if not in good faith, has been raised, although the main suggestion seems to be that where the transaction is onerous the third party should be protected regardless of how the deed is executed.

LEGAL PROCEEDINGS

When trustees bring legal proceedings against a third party, the general rule is that the trustees will be personally liable for any expenses found due to the third party unless the court clearly limits the liability to the trust patrimony. Personal liability arises, once again, because of the fact that the trustees are presumed to know whether the trust patrimony is financially sufficient to meet the costs of any litigation in which they are involved. If the trust lacks the resources to meet these costs, then the trustees must do so out of their own patrimonies.

Where expenses are specifically awarded against a trustee "as trustee", the trustee will not be held personally liable and liability will be limited to the trust estate: *Craig* v *Hogg* (1896). So if a pursuer brings an action against X and Y "as trustees acting under the trust of Z", then it is understood that liability will not extend beyond the trust patrimony: *Mulholland* v *Macfarlane's Trs* (1928). If the action is brought against the trustees as individuals, then the court may expressly award expenses against them personally. In these circumstances, they have no right of relief against the trust estate. However, it is open to them to ask the beneficiaries to indemnify them in relation to the expenses of the case.

The court, under s 34 of the Trusts (Scotland) Act 1921, may direct, where this is reasonable, that the expenses of any application made to it be paid out of the trust estate. This means that the expenses of any party, including the trustees, can be met from the trust patrimony. However, this must be reasonable. If the trustees unreasonably engage in litigation, this section will not protect them from personal liability. Given their duty to preserve the trust estate, for example, the trustees should not dissipate that estate by engaging in unnecessary litigation. If they do, they will be personally liable for the expenses of that litigation.

EXPENSES AND THE RIGHT OF RELIEF

Where expenses are awarded against trustees, this is usually done by making an interlocutor against the named trustees. This means that they are personally liable but have a right of relief against the trust estate. The rule here is that the trustees are entitled to pay these expenses from the trust estate provided that they incurred them in the necessary, proper and reasonable discharge of their duty as trustees. The law seeks to balance the interests of the trustees against those of the beneficiaries. Trustees must be deterred from litigating too readily but encouraged to litigate when this is in the interests of the administration of the trust. A reckless trustee who enters litigation in disregard of his duty, or one who does so obstinately (for instance, in the face of strong legal advice), will be personally liable and unable to use the trust estate to meet the expenses. Where the trustee is at fault and this has brought about the litigation, there will be no right of reimbursement from the trust estate. A trustee whose own negligence leads to litigation will be personally liable for expenses. On the other hand, a trustee acting reasonably, even if the action he brings is unsuccessful, will not be personally liable and will enjoy a right of relief against the trust patrimony: for example, *Cameron* v *Anderson* (1844).

Not every legal question raised by trustees in court will involve a third party. Trustees, for instance, may apply to the court to rule on the interpretation of an unclear provision in the trust deed. In effect, the fault in this case lies not with the trustees but with the truster. The usual rule in such a case is that the trust estate will bear the expenses of all the parties: for example, *Whyte* v *Hamilton* (1881). This rule may also apply if the trustees, on justified grounds, seek guidance from the court on how to administer the trust estate appropriately where there is some reasonable doubt even though the truster was not at fault.

Where a majority of trustees engage in litigation they may make themselves liable to the minority for the latter's share of the expenses if they use their names without consent. The minority can avoid liability by lodging a minute of disclamation: *Fairlie* v *Fairlie's Trs* (1903).

PROPOSED REFORM

In reviewing this area of law, the Scottish Law Commission has made several proposals (Scot Law Com No 148 (2011), para 4.13). First, trustees who raise proceedings should be personally liable for the defender's expenses but have the right to ask the court to exclude personal liability where they can show that the trust assets are sufficient to cover them or that they had obtained security in respect of the payment of expenses. Second, where trustees defend an action, pursuers should have no recourse against their personal patrimonies. Third, if the trustees behave improperly or engage in unnecessary action, the court would be able to impose personal liability on them for expenses and, finally, if equitable to do so, the court could also dispense with personal liability.

Essential Facts

- A trustee who contracts with a third party, when acting within his powers, may be personally liable on the contract unless he makes clear that he is a trustee and that it is the trust patrimony alone that is to be bound.
- The trustee has, in these circumstances, a right of relief against the trust estate in respect of any expenses he has incurred in making the contract.
- A trustee who acts beyond his powers in contracting with a third party will be personally bound and has no right of relief against the trust estate. The contract and any conveyance, depending on the precise power being asserted, may be valid as a result of s 2 of the Trusts (Scotland) Act 1961. This may potentially result in loss to the beneficiary.
- A trustee who enters a contract *ultra vires* and then is in breach of that contract is personally liable and has no right of relief against the trust estate.
- If a trustee carries on a business as part of the administration of the trust, then he will be personally liable for any delicts committed against a third party by himself, or any employee or agent, in the course of that business.
- A deed granted by a quorum of trustees, in pursuance of a resolution they have reached in administering the trust, gains some protection from challenge under s 7 of the Trusts (Scotland) Act 1921 in respect of procedural irregularities by the trustees.

Essential Cases

Cuningham v Montgomerie (1879): trustees were empowered to invest in stocks and securities. They invested in the City of Glasgow Bank, which then failed. The question arose whether they had any personal liability. The court held that there was no personal liability. The trustees were entitled to relief by placing the trust fund between themselves and the bank's liquidators. This was more than mere reimbursement of money spent; the trustees were entitled to relief of obligation.

Mulholland v Macfarlane's Trs (1928): the pursuer won damages against the trustees having suffered injury through being knocked down by a bus belonging to the trustees that was driven by one of their employees. The pursuer sought decree in regard to both damages and the expenses of the action against the trustees as individuals without reference to their office. The court held the trustees liable jointly and severally as individuals for expenses but liable only as trustees for the damages. The summons had referred to three named individuals "as trustees under" the will of the truster. Any limitation of liability inferred from this did not include expenses, because a party is entitled to recover expenses from any party whose interference in litigation has caused him expense, whether or not the party was named in the summons. The general rule, therefore, is that trustees are liable for expenses as principals. However, decree for payment of damages had to pass in terms of the crave of the initial writ, that is against the trustees as trustees, and they were not personally liable. This was despite the fact that the trustees as individuals were *prima facie* liable for the damages in the circumstances; the fact that they were not sued as individuals limited liability to the trust estate.

10 THE TERMINATION OF TRUSTS

There is no rule that requires a trust to terminate. Some public trusts may continue to operate for many years and may even exist in perpetuity. However, most trusts are not intended to last forever and will come to an end. Sometimes the trust will suffer a natural end, with its purposes implemented and all of its funds distributed by the trustees in line with the truster's intention. In other cases, the trust might come to an end prematurely. There are several methods by which this could happen: revocation by the truster; reduction by creditors; or termination by the beneficiaries.

A NATURAL END: TERMINATION BY THE TRUSTEES

Generally, the trustees can only bring a trust to an end by distributing the trust property to the beneficiaries in line with the trust purposes. In the absence of grounds for removal, there is no way of forcing trustees to leave office while assets remain in the trust and the purposes remain unfulfilled. If the purposes can no longer be fulfilled but assets remain, then, for private trusts, there are three possibilities. The purposes will either be varied by application to the court; or there will be a resulting trust in favour of the truster or his heirs; or, if that is excluded by the truster, the trust property will go to whomever the truster nominated in the event of the failure of the purposes.

The trustees have a duty to distribute the trust assets in accordance with the trust purposes. If the trust deed does not make clear how specific assets are to be distributed, then this is a matter for the discretion of the trustees. They must act reasonably and, in particular, they are not entitled to delay payment unless they also have discretion in regard to the date of payment.

In the event that the trustees breach their duty, by distributing the estate to the incorrect person, then the trust is not terminated. The trustees remain bound by their duty to account for trust property. Unless there are grounds on which they can escape liability, they remain under a duty to distribute the value of the estate to the correct payees (be it beneficiaries or creditors). We have already seen above that this is a particularly stringent duty. They may be able to recover payments made in error on the basis of unjustified enrichment. Until they have made good the consequences of their breach of trust, however, the trustees will not be entitled to a discharge.

TERMINATION BY THE TRUSTER

The right of the truster to revoke a trust deed depends on the nature of
the trust.

Testamentary trusts

A testamentary writing may be revoked at any point prior to the death
of the testator. If that writing provides for the creation of a *mortis causa*
trust, therefore, the truster may revoke the trust at any time prior to his
death simply by revoking his will. It makes no difference if he declares that
a testamentary deed is irrevocable or that the deed itself has been shown
or delivered to the beneficiaries. A declaration of irrevocability is simply
incompatible with the nature of a testamentary deed.

It is possible for a testator to bind himself to leave his estate to a particular
person. If such an obligation is made, then it will succeed in being irrevocable. Similarly, a person may contract so that he is bound not to alter
the disposition of his estate: *Paterson* v *Paterson* (1893). This is presumed
to apply only to the estate that is left; it does not prohibit the testator
from alienating parts of his property during his lifetime. If the testator is
bound as the result of a gratuitous unilateral obligation, then this must be
constituted in formal writing under s 1(1) of the Requirements of Writing
(Scotland) Act 1995.

Trusts for administration

A trust for administration (or "bare trust") is a trust which has no purpose
other than to administer property for the truster, or for some other party,
during the truster's lifetime. Maintaining the trust estate is the only purpose
of the trust. Such a trust differs from a standard trust in that the truster is
not divested of trust property. Therefore, the trust estate is available to the
truster's creditors. In this type of trust, the truster can revoke the trust at
any time.

The most common examples of a trust for administration are (a) a trust
set up by a truster who would prefer the property in the trust to be managed
by someone more skilled in property management than himself; and (b) a
trust set up on behalf of a person incapable of managing property himself.

Trusts for creditors

A trust may be created in order to avoid the need for a formal sequestration. The sole purpose would be to ingather the assets for the truster, or
an agreed part of them, to be held in trust for the benefit of the truster's
creditors. This largely, although not entirely, escapes the influence of the

legislation relating to bankruptcy. If sequestration is granted subsequently, the trustee under the deed (who ought to be a qualified insolvency practitioner) is obliged to hand over the estate to the trustee in sequestration. Therefore the initial trust for creditors would effectively be terminated by the award of sequestration.

The right of revocation in other *inter vivos* trusts

Usually in an *inter vivos* trust the truster, having created the trust, disappears from the picture. If he does re-emerge, it will be only because of what is called his "radical right", the ultimate reversionary right, by which, if the trust purposes fail while the trust still has assets (a resulting trust), the trustee will hold the trust for the benefit of the truster and his successors. The precise question of whether or not the trust is otherwise revocable does not, as a matter of fact, arise very often.

As a matter of law, however, whether an *inter vivos* trust is revocable depends on the whether the truster has been divested of trust property in favour of beneficiaries with the intention that this be irrevocable. Such a trust will therefore be irrevocable only where the truster clearly demonstrates the intention that it should be so and effectively divests himself of the trust property.

In general, close examination of the terms of the trust deed will determine the question of whether the trust was intended to be irrevocable. There are several relevant points that might be made. First, in an *inter vivos* trust the presumption will usually be that the truster intends to retain control of his property during his lifetime. There must be evidence to rebut this presumption. Second, a declaration by the truster that the trust is irrevocable is not decisive, although it is strong evidence of irrevocability. It is not decisive because it may run counter to the terms or nature of the deed (a testamentary will is often declared to be irrevocable when, by its nature, it is not). The language used, the nature of the property conveyed in trust and the directions given to the trustees are all evidence from which the intention that the trust be irrevocable may be inferred. On the other hand, if the truster expressly reserves to himself the power to revoke the trust this will conclusively mean that the trust is revocable.

The following three conditions must apply for the trust to be irrevocable:

(1) Title in trust property must have passed to the trustees unconditionally: this means that the "divestiture must be genuine and not simulate" (*Scott* v *Scott* (1930), per LP Clyde). In other words, the transaction must not have an ulterior motive that would negate

the intention of irrevocability. Lord Clyde referred in particular to an *ex facie* absolute disposition with a back bond. This simply means a disposition which looks valid on its face and purports to transfer title unconditionally, however, the back bond is a private agreement between the parties whereby the transferee binds himself to convey the property back to the transferor when a certain contingency is met. The contingency was usually the repayment of a loan and this kind of transaction, represented publicly as a sale from A to B in absolute terms, was actually a loan of money from B to A together with an obligation that B, the secured creditor, would re-convey the property to A once the loan (plus interest) was paid. B got good title to the property but was personally bound not to sell it on to a third party, provided that A fulfilled the conditions of the back bond. The relevance here of such an arrangement is that, if B were a trustee, it could not be inferred that the transfer of title to him by the truster was made with the intention that it be irrevocable.

The truster must be solvent at the date title is transferred to the trustees. This has nothing to do with intention. It relates to the fact that if the truster were insolvent then the transfer of property to trustees may be reduced at the instance of his creditors. As a matter of fact, the creditors would be able to undo the transfer by reducing the conveyance.

(2) There must be ascertainable beneficiaries who are different from the truster: an ascertained beneficiary must exist or, if the beneficiaries are a class, one member of that class must exist. A trust for children as yet unborn, for example, will be revocable by the truster until a child is actually born: *Watt* v *Watson* (1897). Therefore there must not be a trust for administration in which the truster is the beneficiary. That would negate the intention of irrevocability. For so long as there are no ascertainable beneficiaries, the trust will be revocable.

(3) The beneficiaries must have an immediate beneficial interest: a beneficial interest exists where the trustees have a duty to maintain the trust property for the benefit of a beneficiary who may gain a right to immediate possession. This need not be an immediate vested right. It may be an interest that is contingent, such as a legacy subject to a condition that the legatee must reach a certain age. Whether or not the legatee reaches that age is uncertain, but the date on which he would do so is certain (it is a *diem certum*, as the Romans called it). They are regarded as having a right to

benefit that is enforceable against the trustees. A contingency that is wholly uncertain, where gaining a vested interest depends on an event that might or might never happen (such as England winning the football World Cup), will not make the trust irrevocable. In the latter case, all the beneficiary has is a *spes*: a hope that something may occur at an indeterminate time. The trustees have no way of predicting when it might occur and it might never occur.

The rule is that a trust will continue to be revocable where no interest is transferred to the beneficiaries and all they have is a *spes*. The trustees cannot be expected to wait forever to ascertain whether an event that may never happen will actually happen. Requiring them to do so is not consistent with granting an immediate beneficial interest.

TERMINATION BY THE CREDITORS OF THE TRUST

In certain circumstances, a trust can be brought to an end by creditors of the truster. This involves reduction of the trust, rather than revocation. The sequestration of the truster does not mean that a trust is revoked. The trust patrimony is safe from the creditors of the truster and those of the trustees as individuals, provided that the property was properly transferred to the trustees. This, after all, is one of the advantages of the trust. However, in certain circumstances the conveyance of property may be reduced at the instance of the truster's creditors. If this occurs the property will vest in the trustee in sequestration whose role is defined in s 2 of the Bankruptcy (Scotland) Act 1985. The trustee in sequestration is the person appointed, by a sheriff or the Accountant in Bankruptcy, to administer a bankrupt's estate for the benefit of his creditors.

Section 34 of the Bankruptcy (Scotland) Act 1985 deals with gratuitous alienations made by persons who have been sequestrated. Any such alienation by a debtor may be subject to challenge by his creditor or by the trustee in sequestration if it was made within a certain period of the date of sequestration, provided that the debtor was insolvent when he made the alienation. This period is 5 years in the case of alienations to someone who is an "associate" of the debtor (generally, defined in s 74 as a family member, or someone connected by employment or business) and 2 years in the case of other persons. If the challenge succeeds, the court will reduce the alienation.

This is relevant because property alienated may include property which is placed in trust. At the time the alienation is made the debtor must be insolvent (ie his liabilities must exceed his assets), and an alienation to be gratuitous should be made for an inadequate consideration. As well as sales at an undervalue, this includes donations, except for conventional gifts which are reasonable in size and nature, such as modest birthday presents or genuine charitable donations. If the alienation is gratuitous and can be reduced, then the trust will come to an end.

TERMINATION BY THE BENEFICIARIES

There are two circumstances in which the beneficiaries can terminate a trust. The first is the common law principle, already encountered in Chapter 8, by which the beneficiaries may agree unanimously among themselves to bring the trust to an end. Provided that the beneficiaries are capable of consenting, they can collectively ask the trustees to denude office and the trustees, once they have been discharged, must terminate the trust. The second circumstance is a narrower one and it is based on the principle drawn from the case of *Miller's Trs* v *Miller* (1890).

Concurrence of the beneficiaries

The ability of the beneficiaries to agree unanimously among themselves to bring a private trust to an end has already been discussed. The trustees will have no alternative but to accept such an agreement and terminate the trust. They have no ground to object even if terminating the trust is clearly contrary to the interests of the beneficiaries or if the purposes of the trust have not yet been fulfilled.

The same issues of capacity to consent arise on termination as arise in regard to variation of purposes and these have also been discussed previously. Consent by, or on behalf of, all the beneficiaries must be given. If some beneficiaries renounce their rights as beneficiaries, that will not cause the trust to terminate. The trust will continue to be administered on behalf of the remaining beneficiaries.

Alimentary provisions

The concurrence of the beneficiaries to terminate a trust will not lead to the termination of a trust where a beneficiary has entered into the enjoyment of an alimentary provision. This is because of the rule that such a provision cannot be renounced by a beneficiary who enjoys it. However, as was noted earlier, such a provision can be varied under s 1(4) of the Trusts (Scotland) Act 1961.

THE PRINCIPLE IN *MILLER'S TRS* V *MILLER* (1890)

Mackenzie Stuart (at p 353) described this principle in the following terms:

> "when a vested, unqualified, and indefeasible right of fee is given to a beneficiary of full age, he is entitled to payment of the provision notwithstanding any direction to the trustees to retain the capital and to pay over the income periodically, or to apply the capital or income in some way for his benefit".

This needs some explanation. The first point is that the reference to "full age" means 16 years of age. The second point is that the idea of a vested "right of fee" in the beneficiary is problematic: it should be thought of as a vested beneficial interest – a personal right to receive trust property. The third point to make is that the principle does not necessarily mean that the trust comes to an end, unless there is a sole beneficiary. It may continue, once the transfer of property is made to one beneficiary, in regard to other property and other beneficiaries. Fourth, the principle relates only to termination, or partial termination, of a trust and not to variation of the trust.

It is also necessary to note that simply because a beneficiary has a vested indefeasible right to the trust property does not mean that the trustees must terminate the trust and convey trust property to him. They can do so only if the interest of the beneficiary is unqualified. This means that it must not be competing with the original interest of the truster in having the purposes carried out. In other words, the powers remaining to be exercised in the trust must be purely administrative and any dispositive powers held by the trustees must already have been exercised. If that is the case, and all that remains for the trustees is the carrying out of administrative tasks, such as the accumulation of income through the investment and re-investment of trust property, then any further directions by the truster requiring the trustees to retain the trust property for these purely administrative reasons can be ignored.

However, there may be circumstances in which the trustees are entitled not to ignore the truster's further directions and to continue to retain and administer the trust property. For example, if the trustees have entered into obligations for maintaining the estate that might be prejudicial if breached, then they are entitled to fulfil those obligations even if it means that the trust continues and there is a delay in conveying the estate to the beneficiary. Circumstances justifying the trustees retaining the trust property arose in *De Robeck* v *Inland Revenue* (1928). In that case the trustees were executors of an estate that was heavily indebted and in regard to which there were considerable death duties. The trustees agreed with the Inland Revenue to pay the estate duty by instalments over a number of years. The beneficiary of a liferent interest, although she had a vested indefeasible right to income from the estate, was held by the court not to be entitled to force the trustees to terminate the trust because doing that would have incurred liability and prejudiced the administration of the trust.

It will be a question of circumstances whether administrative arrangements made by trustees will entitle them to refuse to terminate the trust and convey the trust property when a beneficiary demands that they do so. The underlying issue is fairness to the trustees, who must not be prejudiced in the proper administration of the trust. If necessary, when making payment to a beneficiary whose right has vested, trustees are entitled to retain sufficient trust assets to carry on the administration of the trust and protect themselves against personal liability. Where the beneficiaries as a whole wish to end the trust and are willing to exonerate and discharge the trustees, then the trustees will have no basis for refusing to terminate and the court will not intervene: *Gray* v *Gray's Trs* (1877).

Finally, although a sole beneficiary may be entitled to terminate the trust immediately and have its property conveyed to him, he is free to choose not to do so. There may be a desire to respect the truster's wishes and to wait for the time the truster thought was appropriate for the distribution of the trust estate to take place.

PARTIAL TERMINATION

Fairness to the remaining beneficiaries is also an issue. If one beneficiary has a vested indefeasible right to a part of the trust property but conveying that part of the property will negatively affect the interest of the other beneficiaries, then the trustees have a right to refuse to make such a conveyance and to maintain the trust as it is. If it is possible to separate one beneficiary's interest while maintaining the remainder of the trust, with no prejudice to the continuing beneficiaries, then this may be done. For instance, if one beneficiary has a vested right but the remaining beneficiaries all have contingent rights which have not yet vested, then it may be possible for payment to be made to the first beneficiary without affecting the interests of the remainder: for example, *Graham's Trs* v *Graham* (1899).

DISCHARGE

The nature and effect of a discharge

A deed of discharge may be granted to an individual trustee or it may refer to a whole body of trustees. Its effect is to protect the trustees from liability from any claim that may arise from their previous acts of administration as trustees or which may arise in future. A discharge is intended to protect them against future personal liability to account to the beneficiaries. This includes personal liability arising from breach of trust and a trustee who is in breach of trust is therefore not entitled to a discharge. However, the discharge itself does not mean that the trust estate is protected against future claims. So, for example, suppose that in a testamentary trust B is entitled under a legacy to £1,000 but the estate has only £600. B may accept the £600 in fulfilment of the legacy and grant a discharge to the trustees. Should further assets in the trust estate be recovered, B would still have a claim for up to £400 in further satisfaction of his entitlement under the legacy. The trustees will have no personal liability but they would be bound to hand over this asset in the trust estate to the proper payee, B, regardless of the discharge. In other words, B's discharge to the trustees cannot be presumed to affect B's entitlement or be taken to mean that he wishes to gift any more assets recovered in the truster's estate to another legatee. Had B received his full entitlement from the trustees, he would not have required to give them a discharge at all. Only a receipt would have been necessary. This is because B, unlike a residuary legatee, has no interest in how the estate was administered, provided that he receives his specific legacy in full. Only the beneficiaries of the whole trust estate, or the residue of the trust estate, will be obliged to grant a general discharge, exonerating the trustees in respect of their administration of the trust.

The grant of a discharge

Unless they are in breach of trust, the trustees are entitled to a discharge either on resignation or when the trust is terminated. If a trustee dies in office, it is his representatives who are entitled to a discharge. Usually it is the beneficiaries who will grant the discharge. In the case of resignation or death, however, the discharge, under s 4(1)(g) of the Trusts (Scotland) Act 1921, may alternatively be granted by co-trustees, provided that the deed of trust says nothing that would prohibit this. Such a discharge will have the same force and effect as a discharge granted by the beneficiaries but it will not bind them if they have a claim against the trustee purportedly discharged. Where a discharge is granted by co-trustees the beneficiaries have the right to challenge it. If it is granted wrongfully, or without reasonable care, then not only is the discharged trustee still liable to account to the beneficiaries, but the trustees who granted the purported discharge may also be liable in damages. Similarly, if the trustees, through fraud or misrepresentation, induce the beneficiaries to grant them a discharge, the discharge may be reduced.

It is open to the truster, in the trust deed, to make provisions about the discharge of trustees. In doing so, he may permit a third party, someone who is not a beneficiary, to grant a discharge. This may be, for example, the parents of a beneficiary who is a child; but it may equally be someone unconnected to the beneficiaries, perhaps a financial expert positioned by the truster to oversee the satisfactory outcome of the trust administration.

In the event that a resigning trustee cannot obtain a discharge from his former co-trustees or from the beneficiaries, he may petition the court for the grant of a judicial discharge under s 18 of the 1921 Act. The court is not bound to grant such a discharge and it has the power to make such enquiry as it thinks necessary before deciding whether to do so. In these circumstances a trustee might have to seek judicial exoneration because of some personal attribute of a beneficiary which precluded him from granting a discharge. For instance, a beneficiary may be a child or may lack the capacity to understand what it means to grant a discharge of liability. Or it may be that no discharge is granted because the beneficiaries are unwilling to do so. They may be concerned about a point of law, or an interpretation of fact, which may lead to a distribution of the estate that is in some way questionable.

When a trust is being wound up, an important element in the granting of a discharge is its timing. When a trust is terminated, trustees are entitled to an unconditional discharge before the final distribution of the assets of the trust. This is the only means they have of placing some pressure on the residuary beneficiaries to grant them a discharge. Once a sufficient discharge is granted, the trustees are bound to distribute the estate and divest themselves of title to it. However, a discharge is restricted to those dealings of which the party granting the discharge is aware at the time it was granted and it covers only what was in the minds of the parties when it was given. Unexpected contingencies, or any intromissions that are hidden and come to light later, for example, are not covered by it.

Form of discharge

A discharge need not be registered in the Books of Council and Session. It need not be written, although, as a matter of good practice, it ought to be made expressly, in writing, and witnessed. It has yet to be determined whether a discharge under the Requirements of Writing (Scotland)

Act 1995 requires to be attested or whether it is sufficient that it bears the signature of the granter. There is authority that conduct may give rise to the inference that the trustees have been discharged: *Scott* v *Mitchell* (1830).

Equivalents to a discharge

Trustees may effectively be discharged without any deed of discharge being given to them. If a beneficiary accepts, for example, some benefit from a trustee or a third party in the knowledge that this is given in order to avoid the trustee having to account to the beneficiary, this might be regarded as the equivalent of a discharge. This is, in effect, personal bar. If a beneficiary, B, accepts a gift from T which is made conditional on B not challenging the administration of a trust, then B would be barred from any such challenge and a discharge would be inferred from his acceptance of the gift.

The limits of a discharge

It has already been noted that a discharge may be open to legal challenge and may be reduced. Moreover, its scope depends on what was known to the party granting it at the time it was granted. If a beneficiary granted a discharge in ignorance of his rights, or when he did not have all the facts before him, then it may be reduced.

To gain proper protection from a discharge, the trustees need to make sure that they have carried out a proper accounting and are entitled to be discharged. They also need to make sure that they have properly identified the parties from whom they should seek a discharge. A discharge from the wrong party is worthless.

A residuary legatee is entitled to offer a discharge in respect of the intromissions of the present trustees only. They will be bound to accept such a discharge and cannot insist that it should also cover their predecessors as trustees: *Mackenzie's Exr* v *Thomson's Trs* (1965). The present trustees have an obligation to account for the intromissions of previous trustees, but this does not make them personally liable for those intromissions (A Mackenzie Stuart, *The Law of Trusts* (1932), p 370).

The grant to the trustees of a valid and full discharge, by those entitled to make it, signals the end of the administration of a trust and the proper end of the trust itself. To maintain the analogy of a trust being born, living and then dying, the discharge constitutes the death certificate.

Essential Facts

- A trust is usually terminated by the discharge of the trustees and the distribution of the estate in accordance with the truster's purposes.
- The truster will usually have the right to revoke a testamentary writing, unless he has bound himself not to do so, and may have the right to revoke an *inter vivos* deed.
- Whether an *inter vivos* trust is revocable depends on the whether the truster has been divested of trust property in favour of beneficiaries with the intention that this be irrevocable.
- To make a trust irrevocable: (a) the truster must have transferred title in trust property unconditionally to the trustees; (b) there must be an ascertainable beneficiary (who is not the truster); and (c) the beneficiary must have an immediate beneficial interest (but not necessarily an immediate vested right).
- The truster's creditors may be able to reduce the trust deed.
- Beneficiaries have a the right to terminate a trust if they all concur in doing so.

Essential Cases

Paterson v Paterson (1893): a mother executed a will in her son's favour in return for certain onerous obligations he had entered into for her benefit. When she died she left a later will in favour of all three of her sons in which she attempted to revoke her earlier testamentary writing. The court held that the revocation was invalid because it was in breach of the testator's contract with her son.

Miller's Trs v Miller (1890): Sir William Miller set up a trust for his son in his will. In terms of the will, the trustees were to transfer the trust property to the son when he reached the age of 25. The trust property was to vest in him when he became 25 or, if he married after attaining the age of 21 with the approval of the trustees, at the date of his marriage, whichever event happened first. After reaching 21, he married with the approval of the trustees. Not satisfied with the allowance paid to him, he claimed that he was entitled to have his share of Sir William's estate conveyed to him without having to wait until he was 25. The court held that he was.

Mackenzie's Exr v Thomson's Trs (1965): an executor raised an action for payment and delivery against trustees of a deceased person's share of the trust estate. The trustees admitted that payment was due but claimed that they were entitled to a discharge not only for their own intromissions with the trust estate but also in regard to those of their predecessors. It was clear that the executor had in mind potential proceedings against the estate of an earlier trustee, then deceased. The court held that the principal obligation of the defenders was to account and, in return for doing so, they were entitled to be protected against claims which could competently be made against them in respect exclusively of their own acts and omissions. The defenders were bound to denude in the pursuer's favour on receiving a discharge in respect of their own acts and intromissions.

Scott v Mitchell (1830): the estate of a man approaching bankruptcy was placed in trust for his creditors. The trustee administered the estate and, after the debtor was bankrupted and died, advertised for his creditors to come forward and divided the estate among them. Scott, alleging herself entitled to the residue, made a claim against the trustees 36 years later. The court held that the trustees were effectively discharged through the inaction of the pursuer.

11 CHARITIES AND CHARITABLE TRUSTS

The law in relation to charities in Scotland was changed significantly by the Charities and Trustee Investment (Scotland) Act 2005. Prior to this legislation, certain public trusts in Scotland had been given charitable status for tax purposes. Those who managed them were subject to particular rules of administration in terms of the Law Reform (Miscellaneous Provisions) (Scotland) Act 1990. Most of this Act has now been repealed. This has had a dramatic effect on the supervision and regulation of charities in Scotland but the tax consequences have seen much less significant change.

CHARITABLE TRUSTS

The term "charitable trust" was used, prior to 1 April 2006, to describe a public trust which had attained charitable status for income tax purposes and which was subject to special rules of administration. These administrative rules were repealed by the 2005 Act.

Public trusts established for charitable purposes still exist and, although many have done so, there is no absolute need for them to seek registration as a charity. However, they cannot describe themselves as a charity without being registered as one and made subject to the supervision of the Office of the Scottish Charity Regulator (OSCR). They do still qualify for tax reliefs. A public trust which has charitable trust purposes is subject to the same rules in regard to the variation and re-organisation of its purposes as any other public trust: s 42(4) of the 2005 Act.

CHARITIES

A charity may be created as a public trust although it can take other forms, including that of company limited by guarantee. There is now a new corporate form which it may take, known as a "Scottish Charitable Incorporated Organisation" (SCIO). The "constitution" of a registered charity includes in its definition both a trust deed and the memorandum and articles of association of a company.

Whatever legal form it takes, as a result of the 2005 Act a charity must be regulated by the OSCR. In order to refer to itself as a "charity", a "charitable body", a "registered charity" or a "charity registered in Scotland", a trust must be entered in the Scottish Charity Register. In order to describe itself as a "Scottish charitable trust", it is now necessary for a trust to enter the Scottish Charity Register.

The OSCR maintains the register and determines who qualifies for registration. Qualification depends on meeting the "charity" test set out in s 7(1) of the 2005 Act. This requires that the purposes of the charity consist of one or more of the charitable purposes and that it provides, or intends to provide, a public benefit in Scotland or elsewhere.

Section 7(2) of the 2005 Act provides a list of 15 charitable purposes. These are drawn quite broadly and include the following:

- the prevention or relief of poverty;
- the advancement of education;
- the advancement of religion;
- the advancement of health;
- the saving of lives;
- the advancement of citizenship or community development;
- the advancement of the arts, heritage, culture or science;
- the advancement of public participation in sport.

A sixteenth purpose is included which is even broader, being defined as "any purpose that may reasonably be regarded as analogous to any of the preceding purposes". Section 7(3) adds further definition to some of the purposes. For example, "sport" is said to mean "sport which involves physical skill and exertion".

It is useful to think of these purposes as being the basis of a "registered charity" and not to confuse them with the law of trusts. It is clear that some of these purposes are far too wide and uncertain to be valid trust purposes in Scots law. A charity may be registered on the basis of the "advancement of religion" but no trust could validly be constituted with a purpose so lacking in specification. However, a public trust for the advancement of education, which is sufficiently certain to be valid, could seek registration as a charity although the trustees are under no obligation to register in this way.

PUBLIC PURPOSE

There is no presumption that any particular purpose must be for the public benefit. In determining whether a body that seeks to be a charity provides or intends to provide a public benefit, the OSCR must, under s 8(2) of the 2005 Act, have regard to the following factors:

(a) how any benefit gained by members of the body or anyone else (other than members of the public) through the body exercising its functions compares with the likely benefit to be gained by the public by that exercise; and

(b) how any disbenefit incurred by the public through the exercise of those functions compares with the benefit likely to be incurred by the public; and

(c) where benefit is likely to be provided to a section of the public only, whether any condition on obtaining that benefit is unduly restrictive.

Point (c) may cover, for example, the payment of fees for independent schools which seek to register as charities.

A public benefit may be direct or indirect. The OSCR gives as one example of indirect benefit a professional body providing training and regulation of professional standards. The individual who is trained gains a direct benefit, but the public at large may gain an indirect benefit through any rise in the standard of care brought about by the training (OSCR, *Meeting the Charity Test*, p 16).

CHARITY TRUSTEES

The term "charity trustees", according to the definition in s 106 of the 2005 Act, refers to those who have the general control and management of a registered charity. This is slightly misleading in the sense that a charity need not be in the form of a trust and, if it is not, the managers of a charity are not "trustees" in any usual legal sense. Indeed, as was noted above, it might in some cases be impossible for a charity to be constituted validly as a trust. If it is not a trust, then the charity may take another form such as that of a company registered by guarantee, or an unincorporated association.

The duties of a charity trustee are set out in s 66 of the 2005 Act. As well as a duty to act in the interests of the charity, he must seek to ensure that the charity acts in a manner consistent with its purposes. The trustees must exercise the care and diligence that it is reasonable to expect of a person who is managing the affairs of another person. There is a duty to disclose any conflict of interest and to decline to participate in any decision where such a conflict exists; there is a clear emphasis on placing the interests of the charity first and before those of the founder of the charity. These duties are in addition to any duties imposed by the common law or by any other statute.

A trustee who is in breach of duty is to be regarded as committing misconduct in the administration of the charity. All the trustees must ensure that any breach of duty is corrected by a trustee guilty of the breach and that any trustee persistently in breach of duty is removed.

Charity trustees may be remunerated if they provide a service to or on behalf of the charity but this is subject to conditions and it must be set out in a written agreement. Before the agreement is made, the charity trustees must be satisfied that it is in the interests of the charity for the services to be provided by the service provider up to the agreed maximum amount of remuneration. This maximum amount must be reasonable and the giving of remuneration must not in itself be prohibited by the charity's constitution. A further condition is that, prior to the agreement being made, less than half of the trustees, or persons connected to them, should have been in receipt of remuneration. "Persons connected" include parents, brothers, children, spouses, civil partners and cohabitees. While it is possible for connected persons to receive remuneration from the charity, this is also subject to conditions.

DISQUALIFICATION OF A CHARITY TRUSTEE

Of particular note are the provisions in s 69 of the 2005 Act which deal with the disqualification of a charity trustee. Anyone convicted of an offence under the 2005 Act, or an offence of dishonesty, is disqualified from acting as a charity trustee, as is any undischarged bankrupt or any person previously removed from the administration of a charity in Scotland or in England and Wales on the basis of misconduct. Disqualified company directors are also prohibited from being charity trustees. The OSCR, on the application of any disqualified person, has the power under s 69(4) to waive the disqualification either generally or in relation to a particular charity or type of charity. Under s 70 it is an offence to act as a charity trustee while disqualified, although any acts done by such a trustee are not invalid simply because he was disqualified.

THE CHARITY REGISTER

The OSCR has a duty to maintain the Scottish Charity Register under s 3 of the 2005 Act. Over 23,000 charities are now registered in Scotland. Each registered charity has a unique entry in the register. A proposal to register a name that is too similar to that of an existing charity will be rejected, under s 10, since it may cause confusion. Similarly, a name likely to mislead the public as to the true purposes of the body applying for registration would also be rejected, as would any name suggesting a link to government. Names which are offensive will be rejected. Once registered, a charity can change its name only with the consent of the OSCR, which may object only if there is a ground to do so under s 10 (ie a similar name, a misleading name, an offensive name or a name suggesting a link to government). The OSCR also has the power to direct that a charity change its name where the name, in the view of the OSCR, is an infringement of s 10.

A body once registered as a charity may, under s 13, refer to itself as a "charity", a "registered charity" or a "charity registered in Scotland". If established under the law of Scotland, or managed mainly in or from Scotland, a charity may refer to itself as a "Scottish charity" or a "registered Scottish charity". Without registration, a charitable trust cannot refer to itself by any of these terms.

The OSCR, under s 21 of the 2005 Act, must make the Scottish Charity Register available for public inspection, so that the information it contains is reasonably obtainable. It has the power to issue a notice to any charity requiring it to provide information and documentation relative to the charity's entry in the register. The entry for each charity must set out the name, address (of the charity or one of its trustees) and purposes of the charity, as well as any other information the OSCR considers appropriate.

OSCR INVESTIGATORY POWERS

Under s 28 of the 2005 Act, the OSCR has extensive powers to make enquiries in regard to any charity or a body which is controlled by a charity. It can also investigate bodies not on the register which appear to represent themselves as charities or any person representing that he works for such a body. When investigating, it has power to direct that activities cease for up to 6 months while the investigation proceeds and it is an offence to fail, without reasonable excuse, to comply with such a direction. In the course of investigating, the OSCR may require by notice that information be given to it if it regards that information as necessary. It is an offence not to supply that information, without reasonable excuse, although the OSCR must pay any reasonable expenses incurred by those supplying it. Confidential information, which would not be required to be disclosed in Court of Session proceedings, is exempt from the requirement of disclosure.

As a result of its investigations, the OSCR may remove a charity from the register if it has found that it no longer meets the "charity" test. If misconduct has been found in the administration of the charity or a body under its control, and it is necessary to do so for the charity's protection, then the OSCR may issue a notice suspending any person concerned in the management or control of the charity, provided that they were aware of the misconduct, or had facilitated it, or they are simply unfit for office. It can also restrict the transactions entered into by the charity or payments made in its administration and it can direct any third party holding property for the charity not to part with that property without the OSCR's consent.

If a body has been representing itself to be a charity when it is not, then the OSCR has the power to direct it to stop making such representations. On this basis it can also restrict the body's transactions.

Following an enquiry which has resulted in action being taken, the OSCR may publish a report under s 33, in such manner as it thinks fit. The report can identify the person in respect of whom enquiries were made.

On the application of the OSCR to the Court of Session, the court has a number of powers under s 34 of the Act where it is satisfied that there has been misconduct and that exercise of the relevant power is necessary for the protection of the property of a charity. The powers include the power to grant interdict, to appoint a trustee or suspend or remove one, and to appoint a judicial factor to manage the affairs of the charity. The court also has powers where it is satisfied that a body has been misrepresenting itself as a charity.

HM REVENUE AND CUSTOMS AND THE OSCR

The details of the tax regime for charitable trusts are beyond the scope of this work. However, trusts established for charitable purposes have for long received favourable tax treatment from HM Revenue and Customs and have the right to seek tax relief. HMRC and the OSCR will generally work together to assist charities, and bodies applying for charitable status, also to qualify for recognition as charities for tax purposes.

Traditionally, tax legislation has defined trusts in terms more recognisable to the law of England and Wales than to Scots law. The 2005 Act has been drafted in similar terms to legislation in England. Registration as a charity automatically brings with it relief from non-domestic rates charged by local authorities. Therefore, if an organisation passed the "charity" test and it is admitted to the register, it gains local tax advantages as well as the advantage of being able to describe itself as a charity. It has been argued that this approach is unnecessarily complicated and that it would be better to divorce liability to supervision entirely from eligibility for tax relief (P Ford, "Supervising Charities: a Scottish-civilian alternative" [2006] 10 Edin LR 352 at 385).

The developing relationship between HMRC and the OSCR will help ensure that new charities in Scotland continue to qualify for tax exemptions and reliefs. Under a Memorandum of Understanding in 2008, the UK tax authorities and the OSCR established a clear basis for the mutual exchange of information. It is the working practice of HMRC that an entry on the Scottish Charity Register, in the vast majority of cases, will satisfy it for the purposes of granting tax relief. This is clear from a separate joint statement, on the definition of "charitable purposes", also issued in 2008.

HMRC and the OSCR have also issued a joint statement in relation to a particular problem that might arise where a charitable body in Scotland, under its constitution, is allowed to distribute any of its property for a non-charitable purpose. Such a body could not be a registered charity. Tax issues would have arisen had this not been the case, since "charitable purposes" was defined in English law differently from the definition in Scots law and the English definition governed the tax treatment of such bodies.

Whether a new charity, or a public trust with charitable purposes, should in future gain charitable tax relief or exemption from tax from the UK tax authorities is less clear than it might have been, given the fact that the definition of "charity" in the 2005 Act is not identical to that in English law. The position of applicants is now subject to a Memorandum of Understanding entered into between HMRC and the OSCR in 2008. This sets out, in para 18, the procedure in the event that an organisation applies to HMRC for charitable tax relief without first having registered in the charity register. HMRC will insist that an organisation has applied to the OSCR for charitable status before it makes an assessment on charitable tax relief. Once the OSCR has made a decision, whether successful or not, HMRC will then make an assessment on charitable tax relief. This would seem to encourage, but not oblige, new charitable trusts in Scotland to register as charities.

DUTY TO PROVIDE ACCOUNTS

A charity must, under s 44 of the 2005 Act, keep proper accounting records and prepare a statement of account in each financial year. The statement must be independently audited and a copy must then be sent to the OSCR. Where the charity fails in this duty, then the OSCR may appoint a suitably qualified person to prepare a statement of account. That person has certain powers, under s 45, in respect of access to documents and information. Failure to comply with the exercise of these powers is an offence. The cost of having someone appointed to carry out this task is something for which the charity trustees are personally liable on a joint and several basis.

Any auditor who becomes aware of any matters in regard to the charity
or any institution or body corporate connected to the charity which may
be relevant to the functions of the OSCR, particularly in terms of its over-
sight of the register, is obliged to report this where he has reasonable cause
to believe it to be of material significance.

SCOTTISH CHARITABLE INCORPORATED ORGANISATION (SCIO)

The 2005 Act created a new corporate legal form which charities may
choose to adopt. This part of the Act, which came into force on 1 April
2011, allows a charity to adopt the form of a corporate body. This mirrors
a similar development in England and Wales. The SCIO provides limited
liability and separate legal identity to organisations that wish to become
charities but want to avoid the complications of company law and there is
no need for an SCIO to register with Companies House.

As a legal entity, an SCIO has the capacity to sue and be sued in its own
name, to make contracts and to employ staff. As a body corporate, it must
have two or more members, under s 49(2), and its constitution must, under
s 50(2)(b), provide for the appointment of three or more charity trustees.
Its membership may consist entirely of its charity trustees. Any document
issued by, or signed on behalf of, an SCIO must state that it is an SCIO.

RE-ORGANISATION OF CHARITIES

Once a charity is registered it cannot change any of its purposes without
the consent of the OSCR: s 16(2)(a). Since a "charity" is defined in s 106
of the Act as a body entered in the Charity Register, then a charitable trust
would not require consent unless it had first been entered in the Charity
Register. The variation of trust purposes in a public trust which is not a
registered charity must still be undertaken by the court. The Scottish Law
Commission has proposed to extend the powers of the OSCR so that it
may vary the purposes of public trusts that are not registered as charities
(see Chapter 8).

Pending any future reform, the rules concerning the re-organisation of
the purposes of a charity under the 2005 Act will apply only where the
trust is on the Charity Register. The 2005 Act does not prejudice the right
of trustees to petition the Court of Session for approval of a *cy-près* scheme,
and that remains as an alternative. However, the procedures set out in ss 9
and 10 of the Law Reform (Miscellaneous Provisions) (Scotland) Act 1990,

discussed in Chapter 8, are not available to trusts that are registered charities. This exclusion is set out in s 15(9)(b) of the 1990 Act.

CONSENT PROCEDURE

An application to re-organise a charity must be brought by charity trustees or someone acting for them, such as a solicitor. However, the OSCR has indicated that it will take a "pragmatic approach". For example, a local authority which governs a charitable trust might be able to apply to the OSCR, particularly where the governance arrangements have become unclear (OSCR, *Consents and Notifications* (2007), para 3.1). In its 2010/11 annual report, the OSCR anticipated a number of re-organisation schemes being put forward by local authorities which administer charitable trusts in order to release additional charitable funds as a response to difficult economic challenges.

A charity requires the consent of the OSCR, under ss 11 and 16, to do any of the following: change its name; amend its constitution in regard to its purposes; amalgamate with another body; wind itself up; or change its legal form. Where the charity has the inherent power to make such a change, the OSCR need simply give its consent (and it may do so subject to conditions or, indeed, refuse to do so). A change to purposes will not take effect unless and until the OSCR has specifically consented. In regard to any other change under s 16, consent is presumed unless it is specifically refused within 28 days. Under s 17 certain other changes need only be notified to the OSCR; for instance, a change of address or a change in the charity's constitution that does not relate to its purposes. Notification must be made within 3 months of the change.

RE-ORGANISATION SCHEMES

If the constitution of the charity does not permit the desired change to be made, then an application for approval of a re-organisation scheme must be made to the OSCR under ss 39–43 of the 2005 Act. A trust deed, for example, will usually not permit the trustees to alter the deed in order to change trust purposes. It is worth repeating that a petition to the Court of Session for approval of a *cy-près* scheme remains a valid alternative to an application for a re-organisation scheme.

A "re-organisation scheme" is a scheme for:

(a) varying the charity's constitution (whether or not in relation to its purposes);

(b) transferring the charity's property to another charity; or

(c) amalgamating the charity with another charity.

A notice of the application for such a scheme will be published on the OSCR website (usually for 28 days but this may extend to 42 days) and, in the case of charities with an annual income of or exceeding £250,000, in a newspaper. Members of the public may lodge objections to the proposals in the application. Once the period for receipt of objections has passed, the OSCR will consider the applications and must determine it within 6 months from the last date on which objections could be received. All the objections received must be considered during this decision-making process.

The grounds on which the OSCR can approve a proposed change depend on whether what is proposed is a change in purposes or a change in some other aspect of the constitution of the charity.

CHANGE OF PURPOSE

Where it is proposed to change the purposes of a charity, the OSCR must consider whether the proposed re-organisation scheme will enable the resources of the charity to be applied to better effect for charitable purposes. This must be done consistently with the spirit of charity's constitution, taking into account changes in social and economic conditions since it was constituted. In addition, one of the following two conditions must be met.

First, some or all of the purposes of the charity must:

(a) have been fulfilled as far as possible or adequately provided for by other means; or

(b) can no longer be given effect to (whether or not in accordance with the directions or spirit of its constitution); or

(c) have ceased to be charitable purposes; or

(d) have ceased in any other way to provide a suitable and effective method of using its property, having regard to the spirit of its constitution.

Or, alternatively, it must be the case that the purposes of the charity provide a use for only part of its property.

Therefore, the OSCR will approve a change of the charity's purposes where the proposed change will apply the charity's property in a better way yet one that still falls within the spirit of the original constitution.

This might mean a new purpose that allows a similar group of people to be assisted, in a similar way to those originally assisted by the charity, so that the assets of the charity can be put to fuller or more beneficial use.

OTHER CHANGES

The OSCR will approve a change to a charity's constitution that does not affect the charity's purposes if it considers that the provision can no longer be given effect to or is otherwise no longer desirable. However, the proposed re-organisation scheme must enable the charity to be administered more effectively. This provision points towards a more administrative change. For example, a requirement in the constitution that charity trustees must meet every calendar month may be inconvenient and unnecessary. It may be argued that a less regular physical meeting would be better for the effective administration of the charity, given the ease of modern communication between trustees.

THE OUTCOME OF THE PROCESS

Once the decision is taken, the charity must be notified. If the scheme is approved it must then be adopted by the charity, and once adoption has taken place the OSCR must be notified. If the proposed scheme is not approved the charity, under s 74 of the 2005 Act, can ask the OSCR to review its decision. If such a review does not change the decision, an appeal can be made to the Scottish Charity Appeals Panel, which may refer the proposal back to OSCR for reconsideration (s 76). There is a final appeal, under s 78, from the Appeals Panel to the Court of Session.

INDEX